A late-n... street in A... ... ...e main
Marquis of Do... ...observed the third
11.30 pm. Imp... one g... ...er of the inn at
to be kept wait...ing,' observed that invaluable chronicler,
Elizabeth Smith. 'Hah, Mr Kilbee – in bed, hah,' said my
Lord when the innkeeper finally emerged. 'You go early to
bed here, Mr Kilbee.' 'People who pay so high for their
land, my Lord,' returned Mr Kilbee, 'had need to be early
in bed and early up.'

For the most part such drama was rare. The main
excitements were the arrival of the coach from Dublin
with its sixteen passengers at 10 am and its return at 1 pm;
the elderly Dr Parsley on his way to school to teach among
other things 'the rule of 3 in fractions'; the carriages
crowding into town on a fine June evening to view the
monthly fashions which had just arrived at Mr Gilholy's,
including two splendid muslin dresses.

But great events did occasionally unfold here. In May
1798 the rebels surged through the street on their way to
burn Blessington House. And forty or so years later Daniel
O'Connell, then at the height of his fame, was a visitor,
but he drove by rapidly, his closed carriage disappointing
the 'mob of the unwashed' who had gathered. Onlookers
got better value at the birthday celebrations of the fourth
marquis in August 184..., when 1,500 tenants and
peasantry gathered for a great banquet involving 'four
bullocks, twenty sheep, lambs and hams and five-hundred
weight of plum pudding'.

The Blessington E... ...1908 illuminates with
fascinating detail the day-to-day life of the town and its
inhabitants.

Kathy Trant

The Blessington Estate 1667-1908

ANVIL BOOKS LIMITED

*For
Anton,
Maurice, Mary-Liz, Nicholas and Barbara
and the next generation of readers –
Michael and Heather*

First published 2004 by
Anvil Books
45 Palmerston Road
Dublin 6

2 4 6 5 3 1

© Text Kathy Trant 2004
© Design and layout Anvil Books 2004

ISDN 1 901737 51 9

Origination by Computertype Limited
Printing by Colour Books Limited

This publication has received support from the Heritage Council
under the 2004 Publications Grant Scheme

৯৯ Contents

ᔰ Illustrations

ॐ Foreword

When I came to live in the Blessington area over three decades ago, a profound change was taking place in Irish society. The steady flight from the land that had begun in Famine days was now being counterbalanced by the increase in the number of suburban families locating in rural areas, especially those close to large urban centres. The new settlers were intensely interested in their surroundings and soon local history groups began to spring up all over the country. I found myself involved in a study of my own local area and the research I undertook was the starting point for this book.

The story of Blessington is inseparably linked with that of the two great Anglo-Irish families who determined its fortunes for almost two hundred and fifty years – the Boyles and the Hills, or the Downshires as the latter were more generally known. Despite the prominent positions held by Michael Boyle, founder of the town – Archbishop of Dublin, Primate Archbishop of Armagh and Lord Chancellor of Ireland – there was little information about him in the standard history books. Gradually however, and from different sources, like pieces of a jigsaw fitting together, his story emerged.

In contrast, the archival material on the Downshires is very rich. Their estate papers are deposited in the Public Record Office of Northern Ireland and so my research involved many early morning trips to catch the Dublin-Belfast train. The excitement of opening documents, some of which had not seen the light of day for over two hundred years, never faltered. Particularly exciting were bundles of 'vouchers', individual payment receipts for work done on the estate, the earliest of which date to the restoration of Blessington House by Wills Hill, the first marquis, in the 1780s. As each piece of fragile paper was unfolded, it was like opening a small window into the life of the ordinary residents of Blessington all those years ago.

There are two sides to the story of Blessington. On one side are the landlords, their agents and the gentry of the neighbourhood. On the other is the 'hidden Ireland' of the strong farmers in the lowlands and the smallholders in the uplands who were the descendants of the displaced native Irish. It was their stories, like that of Peter Fearis who was threatened with the loss of his farm and successfully appealed to the marquis over the head of the agent, and the sad records of the people who disappeared without trace from the estate during the Famine, that interested me most. I came to appreciate the tenacity of the majority of the tenants as they struggled to meet the rent and cling to their holdings from one generation to the next, until eventually in the Land League days they rose and followed the heady call of Davitt and Parnell: 'The land of Ireland for the people of Ireland.'

I hope this book will appeal to amateur and professional historians as well as to the general reader, to the people both here and abroad whose roots are in the Blessington area, and to those of us who have chosen to settle here.

🐦 1 The Struggle for Land

'Land is the permanent source of wealth.'

JOHN MURRAY

Ireland's history is one of successive waves of foreign invaders who came westward in search of land, bringing with them conflict and dispossession. The struggle for land was not just about survival; land was the gateway to power, prestige and wealth. It created over time the landed estate system with its hierarchy of landowner, agent and tenant, a system that, for good or ill, made a lasting impact on Irish history and the Irish economy. It changed the countryside, creating estate towns and villages, walled and wooded demesnes and fields enclosed by fences of thorn and ash. The history of Blessington and its surrounds – the acquiring of land, the building of a big house, the development of an estate town, and the division of the land into holdings of various sizes which were leased to tenants – is a microcosm of the Irish landed estate system, a way of life that lasted until its eventual break-up at the beginning of the twentieth century.

The Milesians, Formorians, Fir Bolg and Tuatha De Danaan are part of a pre-history that is lost in the mists of time. The first people for whom we have written records are the Goidels or Gaels. These were descendants of the Celts, a people who first appeared around 1100 BC and dominated much of central and western Europe until the Roman legions and Germanic tribes pushed them to the western fringes in the first century BC. Their coming to Ireland is obscure but by the early Christian era, their

11

language, laws (the Brehon code) and culture were firmly established. When St Patrick arrived in the fifth century AD, he found a country divided into a large number of autonomous *tuatha*, small communities ruled by an elected *ri* or king; succession did not automatically pass to the eldest son – he was chosen from the extended ruling family. The land was held by the family group or *fine* and normally could not be disposed of outside the group.

Gaelic society was rural and family based; it was also hierarchical. At the top were the *nemed*, the privileged people, who comprised the kings, lords, clerics and poets. Beneath them were the freemen, while at the bottom were tenants-at-will, serfs and slaves. Most occupations, of which farming was the main one, were hereditary. There were no cities or towns and the people lived in scattered farmsteads or raths; the many ringforts found around the country today were once farming homesteads with buildings inside the enclosure for the family and animals. Most date from the early Christian period and some were still in use in the sixteenth century.

The coming of Christianity to Ireland was to have tremendous cultural consequence. Ireland was the first country outside the Roman empire to be converted to the new faith and the merging of Christianity with the Gaelic order was a peaceful and fruitful process. From the fifth to the ninth century, there was a flowering of art and literature, creating masterpieces like the Ardagh Chalice and the Book of Kells. During this period, churches were established in the Blessington area though none of these survive. An early Christian settlement was situated at Burgage, just outside the town, and an impressive granite high cross known as St Mark's, which was relocated in a nearby cemetery when the reservoir was created in the 1930s, is an indication of the wealth of this foundation.[1]

This golden age of monastic culture ended in 795 when the first wave of Vikings attacked the monastery of Lambay Island off the coast of Dublin. At first they were raiders and

1 Cormac's Chapel, Cashel

plunderers, attracted by the wealth of the monasteries, but eventually they became settlers. They intermarried with the native Irish and made their own distinctive contribution to the country, their most enduring legacy being the towns they founded. Dublin, Wexford, Waterford, Cork and Limerick are all Viking in origin.

The Normans, descendants of Vikings who settled in France, conquered England in 1066. Some went westwards to Wales and it was a band of these Cambro-Normans, nearly all related by blood or marriage ties, who responded in 1169 to the call of Dermot MacMurrough, king of Leinster, to help him in a tribal dispute. Dermot had eloped with the wife of Tiernan O'Rourke, a chieftain of Breifne, who was now seeking revenge. In return for his help, Dermot promised Strongbow, leader of the Normans, his daughter in marriage and the kingdom of Leinster after his death. This was, of course, completely contrary to Brehon law as the kingdom was not Dermot's to give away. Nonetheless, when Dermot died a year later, Strongbow

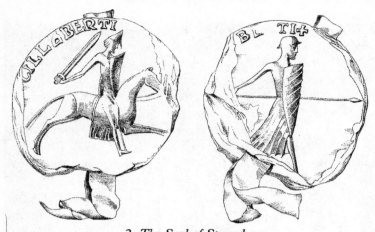

2 *The Seal of Strongbow*

The Pale
Circa 14 88

Ardee
Syddan
Kells
R. Boyne
Drogheda
Athboy
Navan
Trim
Dunshaughlin
Swords
Kilcock
Howth
R. Liffey
Dublin
Tallagh
Clane
Kingstown
R. Dodder
Naas
Kilteel
Saggart
Rathmore
Kilbride
Harristown
Burgage
Ballymore Eustace

- - - The Pale

3 *The Pale circa 1488*

took possession of Leinster. Once they had secured this foothold, the Normans made swift and spectacular progress. Within two years, the Viking cities of Dublin and Waterford had fallen to them and the Gaelic High King of Ireland, Rory O'Connor, had been put to flight. So powerful did they become that their Norman overlord, Henry II of England, who ruled mainly from France and was one of the most powerful monarchs in western Europe at the time, came to Ireland in October 1171 to assert his authority over his Norman barons. In addition, on the foot of the grant of Ireland to the English crown by the Papacy, he managed to gain the submission of most of the native Irish chieftains as well.

In theory at least, Ireland was now an Anglo-Norman lordship, subject to the English king. In reality only the four 'safe' shires of Dublin, Meath, Louth and Kildare, known as the Pale and fortified around its borders, could be counted on as loyal. The rest of the country was classified as 'the land of war'.

The Normans brought with them their own distinctive social, economic and political culture. Their blueprint was the feudal system of medieval Europe, with its emphasis on charters and grants of land in return for homage and military service. It enshrined the right of the eldest son to succeed to his father's property and titles, something unknown in Ireland up to then. Thus their attitude to the ownership and use of land and property was very different from that of the native Irish who still observed the Brehon laws and customs traditional to Gaelic society.

The Normans initially built strongholds – the motte and bailey – from which they made raids on the surrounding area; Rathmore, some kilometres north of Blessington, is a good example of such a defensive settlement.[2] As they became more established through the country, an essential part of their administrative framework was the introduction of the medieval manor and the creation of boroughs or towns. One such borough was created at Burgage. The

Normans continued to prosper and their influence extended north to Inishowen in Donegal and south to Dingle in Kerry. They freely intermarried with the native Irish and adopted many of their customs; some like the de Burgoes of Connacht even spoke Gaelic. In time they formed a ruling caste of powerful families such as the Geraldines and the Butlers who jealously guarded their independence from England. Though in theory they owed allegiance to the English monarchs, the latter were usually too preoccupied with their own problems to interfere. Ireland became in effect a feudal lordship and this remained the situation up to the sixteenth century. A change, however, was at hand. A new dynasty, the Tudors, was on the English throne and Ireland was no longer to be left in the hands of native chiefs or Norman barons.

The first of the Tudors, Henry VII, who reigned from 1485 to 1509, adopted the policy of his predecessors of ruling Ireland through the great Anglo-Norman families, notably the Geraldines or Fitzgeralds, Earls of Kildare, who held the position of king's deputy in Ireland for a long period, representing the visible symbol of English rule in Ireland. The Tudor attitude to the native Irish chieftains was at first conciliatory and a policy of 'surrender and regrant' was put into effect under Henry VIII. The Irish chieftains agreed to recognise the English king as their

4 Henry VII   *5 Henry VIII*   *6 Mary Tudor*

sovereign and surrendered their lands to him. In return they received a charter for their lands and an English peerage, while at the same time promising to pay rents, render military service and promote English law and customs. They also agreed to regard their own kinsmen as vassals under English law and custom.

But the days of the Earls of Kildare as king's deputy were numbered. The tenth earl, Silken Thomas, rose in rebellion and following his defeat he and five uncles were executed in London in 1537. The semi-autonomous lordship of Ireland by the Anglo-Normans, which began with Strongbow's invasion of 1169, was at an end.

7 Silken Thomas at the Council of State

On Henry VIII's death in 1547 a more repressive regime came into power. Two of the midland Irish chieftains, O'Connor and O'More, were goaded into rebellion; it was ruthlessly put down and their lands – part of present-day Laois and Offaly – were confiscated under Mary Tudor in 1556 and given to loyal English tenants. Disaffection with the English Crown was not, however, confined to the native Irish. Between 1569 and 1583 two members of the Geraldine dynasty, James Fitzmaurice Fitzgerald and the

8 Sir Henry Sidney, Elizabeth's Lord Deputy

Earl of Desmond, led a rebellion in Munster. This rebellion was also suppressed, this time by Elizabeth who had come to the throne in 1558. Munster was subdued and 300,000 acres, mostly in the west of the province, were divided into estates of 4,000 to 12,000 acres and parcelled out to 'undertakers', who undertook to attract colonist families to settle on each estate.

The plantation policy which had begun with Mary and continued by Elizabeth's Plantation of Munster of 1586 set the pattern for the future. For the next hundred and fifty years, Irish history becomes a litany of rebellions, suppressions, confiscation of land and resettlement. After the unsuccessful rebellion of O'Neill and O'Donnell, which resulted in the 'Flight of the Earls', James I created the Ulster Plantation. The Rebellion of 1641, which ended with Cromwell's coming to Ireland, resulted in the Cromwellian Settlement.[3] More confiscations followed after the defeat of James II at the Battle of the Boyne, the 'Flight of the Wild Geese' and the Treaty of Limerick.

But a new factor had entered the equation with the coming of Elizabeth I to the English throne. Thereafter, England adopted the Protestant religion while Ireland remained largely Catholic. The new settlers in addition to having a different culture were now of a different religious persuasion and the intermingling of race, which had happened in the days of the Vikings and the Normans no longer took place. Families who wanted to retain their lands and compete for positions of power and influence found it expedient to convert to the new religion. A few, like the Earls of Kenmare, managed to retain both land and religion, but the bulk of the population became second-class citizens. Before the Cromwelliam plantation, Catholics held 60 per cent of the land of Ireland; by 1700 this had dropped to twenty per cent

9 *Elizabeth I*   10 *James I*   11 *Oliver Cromwell*

The plantations had only mixed success. Those who settled in Ireland had to contend with the resentment (which could spill over into violence) of the owners they had dispossessed and the difficulty of attracting or keeping tenants, many of whom returned to England. A significant number did not take up the lands they had been granted; they sold them, thus enabling anyone who wanted a stake in Ireland to build up huge holdings. Some of the native Irish and descendants of the Normans managed to reclaim their lands in this way, while the shortage of eligible tenants meant that others stayed on to work the land they had once owned. But although the century and a half of conflict and confiscation may not have achieved the desired result of transforming a rebel Irish state into a loyal English colony, a new order was now in place that would determine the ownership and use of land for the next two centuries – the landed estate system.

The most obvious characteristic of the landed estate system was the landlord's big house with its adjoining parkland and demesne – features that still survive in the Irish landscape. The landowners, mainly English and Protestant, were a small minority of the population but they dominated all aspects of the life of the people. They regulated the leases and rents under which the tenants held their land and they were also influential in making decisions regarding the construction of roads, canals and railways, as well as playing an important role in the development of towns. Furthermore, they or their agents acted as local magistrates, thereby enforcing law and order and adjudicating in disputes. Until the end of the nineteenth century, the landlords were a powerful and pervasive influence in the life of the majority of the people of the country. At a social level, the hierarchy of titles among the landlords – dukes, marquises, earls and viscounts – defined and preserved the different layers in society. Their educational background set them apart, most of them having attended elitist schools that prepared them for public life. They dominated the Government and monopolised important posts, while the army, church, law and civil service were the favoured occupations for their younger sons. In this way the landowners formed a hegemony that protected their interests in all walks of life. By the end of the eighteenth century their position was secure from contest. The changeover from insecure invaders existing behind fortified walls to country aristocracy living luxuriously in landscaped estates had been accomplished.

The landowning class, however, was not a homogenous group but consisted of different social layers. In Ireland, at the bottom of the group were about 15,000 owners of

12 Carrickfergus Castle

13 The Edgeworthstown estate

estates of less than 1,000 acres. These generally lived on their land and while important in their own localities as resident gentry were socially not greatly different from large tenant farmers. A smaller group, about 3,400 families, owned estates of between 1,000 and 10,000 acres and above them was an even more select group of approximately 300 families, owning estates in excess of 10,000 acres. This latter group was the cream of Irish society and included the Dukes of Leinster, descendants of the Norman family of Fitzgerald, the Earls of Inchiquin who claimed descent from Brian Boru of the Gaelic O'Brien clan, and the Earls of Cork from the era of the plantations. To this group also belonged the two families associated with the Blessington estate – the Boyles, who became Barons and later Viscounts of Blessington, and the Hills, who were to assemble an array of titles culminating in that of Marquis of Downshire.

🪶 2 The Boyle Dynasty

*'Do not do to others what you do not
wish done to yourself.'*

BOYLE FAMILY MOTTO

The Boyle dynasty began with Richard Boyle, who was born of yeoman stock in Canterbury, England, in 1566. Before he was twenty years old he had made his way to London where he acquired some legal and secretarial skills. In Ireland, the Desmond rebellion in Munster had been savagely suppressed and vast amounts of land belonging to the rebels were confiscated, and divided among new settlers and undertakers. It was not a seamless transition. Irish families who had been loyal to the Crown and fought against the rebels sought to retain their estates, while many of those who had been allocated land wanted to sell rather than to settle in Ireland. Men with legal training were urgently required to sort out claims and confer title to the confiscated land. Thus it was that Richard Boyle arrived in Cork in 1588, with '£27 3s in money, a diamond ring and a bracelet, and his wearing apparel', and ended up as the richest landowner in Ireland.[1]

He began by working for the Crown, investigating land titles in Munster and Connacht. At the same time he was acquiring land for himself and this was later to be questioned on the grounds that as an insider he was able to procure title to Crown land at low rates. The matter might have had serious repercussions for him had he not had the support of important people at court. He forfeited the land he had acquired but quickly made good the loss, this time by buying the 12,000 acre estate of Sir Walter Raleigh in

14 Richard Boyle, Earl of Cork

counties Waterford, Cork and Tipperary for the even then
paltry sum of £1,000. The manner of this acquisition,
which happened after the arrest of Raleigh in 1602 when
the family was in penury, was to haunt Boyle for life.
Although Raleigh himself seems to have borne him no
grudge and indeed later defended him against accusations
of fast dealing, Lady Raleigh believed that Boyle had taken
advantage of the family's situation. She kept the issue alive
throughout her lifetime, thus giving fuel to Boyle's many
detractors, of which Thomas Wentworth, later Earl of
Strafford and Lord Deputy of Ireland, was the most
powerful and dangerous.[2]

Even in his own day, Boyle's meteoric rise from obscure
legal clerk to enormous wealth – he was reputed to be worth
£20,000 a year in 1641 – was without parallel and caused
resentment among the older established families. A com-

plex and pious man, he held the view that his wealth and possessions had come to him through the direct involvement of providence in his affairs. His motto 'God's Providence Is Mine Inheritance', chosen when he was created Earl of Cork in 1620, sums up this belief.[3]

According to his biographer, Nicholas Canny, he cherished his wealth 'to honour God, serve the king, strengthen the commonwealth and enhance the reputation of his family and posterity'. Wealth and title alone did not automatically secure social acceptance; that came mainly through the time-honoured route of well-connected marriages. His second, to Catherine, daughter of Sir Geoffrey Fenton, whom he described as 'the crown of all my blessings', opened doors in Irish society, although it was not until much later, and especially after he became a member of the English Privy Council, that he was finally accepted into the upper ranks of English society. Equally influential marriages for members of his numerous family (seven sons and eight daughters) were pivotal to his plans. He was renowned for the extravagant settlements he made on them and in many instances his financial commitment extended beyond the initial marriage contracts.

His crowning achievement was the marriage of his daughter Joan to George Fitzgerald, sixteenth Earl of Kildare, in 1629. The young earl led a dissolute life and

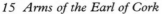

15 *Arms of the Earl of Cork*   16 *Kildare coat of arms*

his estate was severely encumbered but Boyle knew that an alliance with one of Ireland's noble families would secure him the place in Irish society he craved. He rebuilt the Fitzgerald castle at Maynooth, which was almost in ruins and lacked plate, hangings and utensils, and also restored the adjoining church. The official opening took place without the attendance of his son-in-law, with Boyle himself taking the place of honour alongside his daughter. He increasingly took over the management of the mortgaged Kildare estate, much to the chagrin of the young earl, who cannot have been too pleased that the Boyle crest was now displayed beside that of the Fitzgeralds over the entrance to the castle, and who increasingly found himself reduced to an appendage in his own household.[4]

Until Boyle had established himself in the social hierarchy, he was to a great extent isolated on his Irish estates, an unknown Englishman in a foreign country. It was important for him, therefore, to have kinsmen nearby who would give him unqualified loyalty, and so he invited relatives to join him in Ireland, offering them a share in his wealth and prestige. One of these was his cousin and namesake, Richard Boyle, who had been a teacher in Barnett at a salary of £20 per annum. He was given the Deanship of Lismore and later elevated to the See of Cork; in the climate of the age it was prudent to have trustworthy friends not only in secular but also in ecclesiastical positions of strategic importance. The newly appointed Bishop of Cork, however, was a man who did not always toe the family line. In a dispute between his cousin, the Earl of Cork, and Thomas Wentworth, the Lord Deputy, the bishop sided with Wentworth. In the ensuing fallout, he found it expedient to put himself beyond the reach of his irate cousin and with the help of Wentworth he transferred to the Archbishopric of Tuam.[5] It was his son, Michael, who was to be granted the Lordship of Blessington later in the century.

Michael Boyle was born about 1615, the eldest son of a

17 Archbishop Michael Boyle

family of two sons and nine daughters, and died at the venerable age of 87 in 1702.[6] He was educated at Trinity College, where he received an MA and a DD (he was later to give the college £200 towards the cost of the front gates). In 1637, he obtained a rectory in the diocese of Cloyne, county Cork, and became dean in 1640.

Resentment against English rule was simmering below the surface and when the Rebellion of 1641 broke out Boyle and his family felt the consequences. His appointment as chaplain-general to the English army in Munster was overshadowed by disasters. His first wife Margaret and their only child Martha, as well as his wife's mother, grandmother and great-grandmother, were lost 'at sea upon ye flight out of Ireland' to escape the fury of the rebellion. Two children of his sister Anne were also lost at sea at this time, while a brother-in-law, the Dean of Cork, died in

Bristol. Another brother-in-law was killed 'in ye king's service by ye rebels'. In October 1642, the long-running feud between King and Parliament erupted in civil war in England, leading to a realignment of the different factions in Ireland, with the rebels of 1641 joining the forces of Charles 1 to fight the Parliamentarians. The Civil War ended in England in 1648 and Charles 1 was executed the following January, the year in which Cromwell came to Ireland to stamp out both royalists and rebels. This resulted in the death of Boyle's only brother, Richard, who was 'barbarously murdered by Cromwell at Drogheda in Ireland in cold blood and two days after [the] usurper had taken ye citty from ye kings force, *anno* 1649'.[7]

18   Cromwell at Drogheda

The complex and changing situation in Ireland in the seventeenth century, when survival depended on the ability to foresee how the political wind was blowing and religious and civil allegiances could often change, is reflected in the life of Morough O'Brien, first Earl of Inchiquin, into whose family Boyle was later to marry. As a royal ward, Morough converted to Protestantism around 1630 and in the Rebellion of 1641 fought initially on the royalist side. As the Civil War in England progressed he was drawn to the Parliamentarians and won a decisive battle for them at Knocknanuss in county Cork. He subsequently rejoined the royalist side but following the collapse of the royalist cause he went into exile where for a time he became governor of Catalonia and converted back to Catholicism. He returned to Ireland in 1663 and was restored to his estates in Munster.

Michael Boyle was not just a leading cleric; he was also active in public life. In 1650 he was among a small group selected by the Protestant royalists to treat on their behalf with Oliver Cromwell, and on the Restoration of Charles II in 1660 he was a member of the delegation that went to London to negotiate a bill for settling affairs in Ireland. In this latter capacity he had a part in framing the Act of Settlement under which title to land in the country was re-established, and many estates up to the beginning of the

19 The Coronation of Charles II at Scone

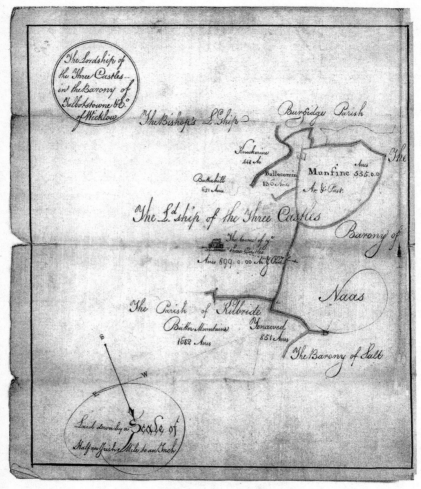

The Lordship of
the Three Castles
in the Barony of
Ballotstowne &c.
of Wicklow

The Bishop's L. Ship

Burbidge Parish

Knockerine
444 A

Butterhill
651 Acres

Ballecomm
130 Acr

Munfine 535.0.0
Ar. & Past.

The

The L. ship of the Three Castles

Barony of

The towne of y
Three Castles
Acres 899-0-00 Ar. & Past.

Naas

The Parish of Kilbride
(Butter Mountains)
1682 Acres

Venarved
851 Acres

The Barony of Salt

Laid downe by a Scale of
Half an English Mile to an Inch.

20 *The Lordship of the Three Castles*

twentieth century derived their title from this act. Boyle's
secular and ecclesiastical honours proceeded in tandem. He
was elevated to the bishopric of Cork, Cloyne and Ross in
1660; three years later he transferred to the See of Dublin.
In 1678 he was appointed Primate Archbishop of Armagh.
He became a privy councillor in Ireland under Charles,

held the position of Lord Justice and was Lord Chancellor from 1665 to 1686.

The Restoration of Charles II was followed by twenty-five years of uneasy peace between the new settlers and the disaffected Irish. Despite all this it was for the most part a period of economic expansion. Trade improved, the population increased and Dublin, Cork and Limerick prospered. Boyle was quick to realise the opportunity presented by the redistribution of land. Two weeks after the Restoration, 'hearing that there is a sequestration upon the estates of Colonel Hunkes, John Cooke and several others', he successfully sought a tenancy of Monkstown in county Cork, the lands in question being located 'conveniently for his near residence upon his parish'.[8] In 1667, four years after his transfer to Dublin he bought for £1,000 the old Norman Lordship of the Three Castles in west Wicklow, thirty kilometres south-west of the city, as well as an estate in another Monkstown, this time in south Dublin.[9] Both estates had previously belonged to the Cheevers, a county Meath Anglo-Norman family.

Boyle selected his Wicklow estate as his place of residence and was granted a royal charter to establish a new town, which he named Blessington – or Blesinton as it was more usually called in the seventeenth, eighteenth and nineteenth centuries. Built in the ancient townland of Munfine, it was granted borough status and was to 'extend into the said county of Wicklow every way from the middle of the said town two hundred or more acres in the whole'.[10] According to its charter a sovereign,[11] two bailiffs and twelve burgesses were to be appointed 'in succession forever' and the town was given the right to hold courts of law and return two members to parliament, which it did until the Act of Union united the English and Irish parliaments in January 1801. There is no indication that Blessington's corporation continued after its initial inauguration and the town never attained the importance envisaged by Boyle.

Work on the building of a brick mansion commenced in 1673, to a design by Thomas Lucas, a Dublin architect and carpenter, who had previously worked on St Patrick's Cathedral and on a building in Trinity College. The work was 'to be done exactly according to the draught of the same house made by said Lucas'. Lucas was also responsible for the interior and Thomas Browne, a Dublin mason, was assigned to do the masonry work. The agreements between Boyle and his contractors specified that the two-storied house, built of lime, stone, brick and sand, was to be 106 feet long, 61 feet wide, with walls at least 10 feet high and a cellar 60 feet long and 28 feet wide. The building had a recessed centre at the back and eight dormers on the roof, and like many of the houses of the period the principal rooms were on the first floor. Lucas's contract was for £1,300 and Browne was to be paid £600, but additional expenses and furnishings added considerably to the cost.[12] It was a big financial undertaking and it is no wonder that around this time Boyle, as Chancellor, sought from Thomas Osborne, the Lord High Treasurer, an increase in his salary from £2,000 to £3,000 a year.[13] Whether his request was granted is not known, but the house when completed was described by Samuel Molyneux, as 'very great and beautiful ... in short much beyond any seat in all respects that I have seen in this kingdom'.[14] Maurice Craig, a modern architectural historian, concurs with this and says Boyle's mansion 'must have been among the very finest' of the wide-eaved houses typical of the period.[15]

The demesne and deerpark, richly planted with a variety of trees, extended to over 440 Irish acres.[16] The landscaping was typical seventeenth century, with ponds, canals and a formal garden, and the house provided the focal point on which a network of avenues converged in a 'crow's foot' pattern.[17] One of the main avenues linked the house to the town and St Mary's Church and was in use until recently, while traces of others can be detected in the landscape.

21 Blessington House

Blessington House was similar in style to a mansion built about forty years earlier at Old Bawn in Tallaght by Archdeacon William Bulkeley, a son of a former archbishop of Dublin.[18] This style of dwelling, with extensive windows and spacious interior, had replaced the earlier tower houses of the fifteenth and sixteenth centuries, which had been built mainly with defence in mind. The new style was a sign of the growing security felt by the settlers as the seventeenth century progressed.

When Blessington House was finished, Boyle turned his attention to the building of St Mary's Church, the only extant building in the town associated with him. He was present for the dedication on 17 September 1683, accompanied by the Bishop of Kildare, as well as many of the clergy of the diocese who 'came in their formalities to the church ... most of them in their surplices and hoods' to join the rector, John Sydall, members of the vestry committee including John Finnemore of Ballyward and George Heighington of Donard, church wardens Martyn Rainsford and Joseph Harding, and the parishioners.[19] The procession outside the building was curtailed because of a 'deluge' of rain, which forced the dignitaries to take shelter inside where the formal service of convocation and communion took place.

22 St Mary's Church   *23 The Boyle Memorial*

A memorial erected by his son Morough, Viscount Blessington, which is still to be seen in the chancel of St Mary's, commemorates the archbishop's gift to the town. In addition to building the church and cemetery at his own cost for 'the Glory of God, and the becoming celebration of Divine Worship', he donated 'flagons, chalices, and patens of silver' as well as the 'six harmonious bells', which are one of Blessington's most prized possessions.[20] They are celebrated in an old saying, 'there is nothing to equal the building at Jigginstown,[21] the wells of Tipper and the bells of Blessington', and bear the coat of arms of Archbishop Boyle and the date 1682. As early as 1698, the sexton's duties included the ringing of the morning and evening bells 'at such times as are and have been appointed for that purpose', but the occasions on which the bells were rung were limited. In 1723 it was stipulated 'that there shall be but ffour days allowed ringing days' in the year, for which 'three shillings only each day' was paid, but by 1725 the annual payment to the bell-ringer had been reduced to ten shillings. The repair of the bells was generally contracted for a period of twenty-one years and in 1736 the contractor, John Hoyle, was given an ultimatum to improve his service 'or else forfeit his salary'.

The first person to be buried in the church was the sovereign of Boyle's new town, Philip Pakenham, who had 'dyed at Dublin of a feavour the 28th December 1683 and was buried in the church of Blesinton, his corpse being attended thither with a handsome and decent funerall', at which the Dean of St Patrick's, Dr John Worth, preached the sermon.[22]

How much the archbishop used his Blessington mansion is unknown. He was in residence there in 1678, the year he was promoted to the See of Armagh, taking 'a little air, as physic to prepare more against the next term' and attending to business matters. He had an interest in promoting the growth of flax and one of his letters from Blessington concerned the difficulties the linen industry was experiencing; despite having a ready market for its products, a business set up by Colonel Laurence, in Chapelizod near Dublin, had failed.[23] That same year, the 'Popish Plot', an alleged English Catholic conspiracy to assassinate Charles II, alarmed the Protestant administration in Ireland. Boyle wrote at this time to the Lord Deputy, the Earl of Ormond, warning him that not alone were internal forces threatening the peace of the country but rumours abounded that the French king was about to send troops to assist the Catholic cause.[24] He noted that arms and ammunition were being sent from London to defend the country; '2,000 men well armed' were expected daily, and all the principal towns were 'as well fenced as the standing army and militia can make them ... and all markets are removed without the walls that there may be noe apprehension of danger'. To secure the towns further, all Catholics were disarmed except 'such as are particularly lycenced'. Boyle was worried about the number of 'Papists' who, despite being expelled, had returned, and he blamed much of this on 'ye English themselves ... they know not well how to live without them. They wanted servants; they wanted tenants and they wanted tradesmen ... and the Irish Papists supply them with all these'. Many priests still remained in the country and continued 'to influence the people into rebellion ye first opportunity'. The chiefs of the Gaelic 'septs' were another source of worry and although some might not 'easily adventure into rebellion', numerous followers might become 'tories' and band together to harass the new colonists.[25]

In this climate of fear and mistrust, Boyle himself was not above suspicion. His past association with Colonel Fitzpatricke, a Catholic relative of his wife, led to the accusation that he was 'a great favourer of the papists'. When told of this by his kinswomen, Lady Ranelagh, he strongly defended his position. Referring to the accusation as 'a scandal which I disdayne to answere', he pointed out that his whole life 'from my youth up until this day' had been a constant uninterrupted testimony against the interest of Catholics. 'Few sober men designe against their own interests,' he argued, pointing out that whatever 'little fortune' he had accumulated to support his 'many children, relatives and friends' depended upon the acts of land settlement, which he himself had helped to bring about. It would be madness for him, therefore, at this time of his life ('being about 64 years old') to expect better provision under an 'Irish-papist interest than I now enjoy'.[26]

Boyle's dual role of primate and chancellor also provided ammunition to his enemies. The matter was raised in the House of Lords at Westminster in 1679 – the year after his appointment to Armagh – when concern was expressed that all 'the greate charges of Church and State' were increasingly vested in Boyle's family; this concern was heightened by Boyle's attempt to have his son-in-law, Sir William Davys, appointed Lord Chief Justice. Boyle argued that in all his years as chancellor no complaints had ever arisen and that in any case the combination of both offices has been 'very frequent' in the past. But the unease about Boyle's family securing state positions for themselves was justified. Davys held many official positions throughout his lifetime – Secretary of State, Clerk of the Privy Council as well as Lord Chief Justice. Boyle's son, Morough, was appointed to the Privy Council in 1675 and for a two-week period in 1696 was Lord Justice. Boyle himself continued as Lord Chancellor until 1686 but was the last person in Ireland to hold the position concurrently with that of Primate Archbishop of Armagh.

24 James II landing at Kinsale

The accession of a Catholic king, James II, in 1685 initially raised hopes in Ireland, but James was too anxious to placate his Protestant subjects to alter the *status quo*. His forbearance was in vain. The birth in 1688 of a royal heir raised the spectre of a continuing Catholic dynasty and proved too much for a number of English nobles who invited William of Orange, James's Dutch son-in-law, to take the throne. James fled to France but returned to

25 *James II*   26 *William of Orange*

Ireland the following year at the head of a French army.
Expectations were now high and the country was in
ferment. James summoned the 'Patriot Parliament',
comprised mainly of Catholics, to sit in Dublin that year
and although a number of Protestant bishops attended,
Boyle was not among them, having been 'formally excused
because of sickness and old age'.[27] He also had pressing
personal matters to attend to; Blessington had been
attacked by a horde of wandering rapparees[28] and his
mansion plundered. The archbishop himself had to seek
refuge across the water in Chester.[29] A detachment of
dragoons was then positioned in the town.

William of Orange came to Ireland in 1690 and in July,
at the Battle of the Boyne, won a decisive victory over
James, who once again sought refuge in France. One of
William's Dutch generals, Ginkle, continued the war in
Ireland and in November, Boyle, now back in Dublin,
wrote to his son Morough in London that the tories were
taking advantage of the long nights to harrass and make
'inroads upon the English quarter, to the great terrour and
disturbances of the country inhabitants'. Phillipstown
(present-day Tullamore) was burnt and the garrison forced

to retreat and it was feared that there would be an attack on
Mountmellick. But Queen's county (present-day Laois)
contained so many English planters and was so well
garrisoned it was hoped it would be safe from attack.[30]

A small detachment of Ginkle's 'French troops'
(probably Huguenots fighting with the Dutch) was
quartered in Blessington House, fourteen or fifteen troopers
with their horses in the stables, the commanding officer in
the house. Boyle reported that they were more 'formidable'
than the dragoons who had been there before them, and
'hath put the place and people' into a 'quiet'. The officer in
charge called on Boyle in Dublin to assure him that 'a
tickett' would be given for any hay or oats used by his men,
that the troopers would be banned from going into the park
or 'doing any disturbances to the deer or any [of] my stock
upon the place', that no young trees or hedges in the
demesne would be cut down and that Boyle's labourers
would not be interfered with. In spite of these assurances,

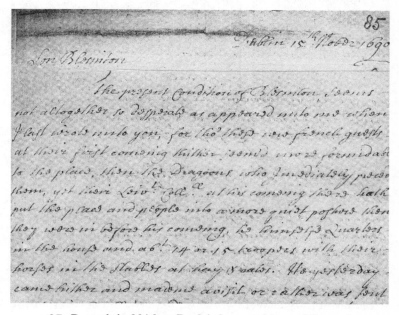

27   Part of Archbishop Boyle's letter to his son Morough

Boyle was concerned enough about his property to ask 'my Lord Justice Sydney' to speak to Ginkle on 'behalf of Blesinton'. A week later he reported to his son that the French troops were still there, although the chief officers were very civil and had not hindered him 'from bringing hither [to Dublin] some small provisions for my family'. He was now worried about reports from his Monkstown estate in Cork, which 'is exceeding spoilt, Red Abbey almost quite destroyed'. He feared that other areas would be left uninhabited and things in general will 'rather grow worse than better this winter'.[31]

28 *Arms of Armagh*   29 *The Blessington arms*

Boyle lived for a further twelve years. He died in Oxmanton near Dublin in 1702 and was buried 'near my dearly beloved wife' in the tomb of his cousin, the Earl of Cork, in St Patrick's Cathedral rather than in the church he himself had built in Blessington, or in Armagh where he was Primate Archbishop. In accordance with his wishes, Archbishop Boyle's funeral took place privately 'without escutcheons or banners'.[32] The tomb is beneath the high altar but the monument, which was originally erected over it by the earl in memory of his wife, was moved on the orders of Thomas Wentworth and is now at the back of the church. There is no inscription on the monument to Boyle's memory, nor to his son and grandson, Morough and Charles, who are also buried in the tomb.

Michael Boyle's second wife was Mary O'Brien, the daughter of Lord Inchiquin, a member of one of Ireland's oldest Gaelic dynasties. They had a large family of nine children – six daughters and three sons. The eldest son, Morough, for whom his father had obtained the titles Baron Boyle and Viscount Blessington, specific to the 'heirs male of the body of his father', inherited the Boyle estates. Two other sons, Michael and Richard, as well as a daughter, Mary, never married and may have died young. The other daughters all made advantageous marriages: Martha to Sir William Davys, son of Paul Davys, Secretary of State and one of the commissioners who had negotiated the Act of Settlement; Elizabeth to Denny Muschamp, whose descendants became the de Vesci family; Honora to Francis Cuffe, whose grandson was Lord Longford; Margaret to Dean Samuel Synge; and Eleanor to William Hill, of Hillsborough in county Down. It was Eleanor's great-grandson, Wills Hill, the first Marquis of Downshire, who eventually inherited the Blessington estate.[33]

The continuity of any family, however great, depends on heirs but in this respect the family of Archbishop Boyle was singularly unfortunate. George Stokes, a nineteenth-century historian, writing about Boyle's estate in Monkstown, county Dublin, which originally had belonged to the Cistercians until the dissolution of the monasteries under Henry VIII, claimed 'that ill luck evermore haunted the families of those who received grants of abbey lands' and this ill-luck was said to manifest itself in a failure to produce male heirs. The same view was held by Archbishop Marsh, the founder of Marsh's Library in Dublin, who was always careful never to purchase confiscated monastic land, and also by Jonathan Swift who was said to be of like mind.[34] Whatever the reason, the male line of the Boyle family died out in three generations.

Morough Boyle, who was born in Cork in 1648 and educated at Trinity College, Dublin, was for a short period in the 1660s MP for Kilmallock. He became a member of the Privy Council in June 1675 and Governor of Limerick and Constable of Limerick Castle in the years 1678-1692.[35] He also had literary leanings and wrote a tragedy, *The Lost Princess*, which a critic of the day felt 'did no credit to the name of Boyle'.[36] Monkstown Castle, considered one of the finest residences in south Dublin, was refurbished by Morough and contained a library and chapel, as well as a fernery and ice-house in the gardens.[37] His interest in the Blessington estate is uncertain but the fact that his chaplain, Monsieur Gilmud, died in the town in 1710 suggests that Morough lived there, at least for some time.[38]

Like his father, Morough married twice. His first wife Mary, daughter of Archbishop Parker of Dublin, bore him one child, a daughter Mary, who married Sir John Dillon. His second wife, Lady Anne Coote, daughter of the Earl of Mountrath, bore him four children, two boys and two girls. The eldest son, Michael, died young and without issue. Charles married first his cousin Rose Coote who died without issue, and then Martha Matthews of Bennetstown, county Kilkenny, by whom he had a son who died in infancy in 1710.[39] Alicia's marriage to Sir Pierce Butler, Viscount Ikerine, and Anne's to William Stewart, Viscount Mountjoy, both produced children but Alicia's only son, James, died at the age of thirteen. So of Morough's children, only Mary's daughter and a son and daughter of Anne survived to the next generation.[40]

Some years before his death in 1718, Morough, who was concerned that Charles had not provided an heir, specified in his will that 'in order to continue the lands' at Blessington and Monkstown 'in the blood and family of the said Viscount Blessington', the estate was to be settled firstly on his daughter Anne and her heirs, and if that line failed on Mary Dunbar, the daughter of his eldest child Mary Dillon. Charles, who spent much of his time in

30 Monkstown Castle

France and died there in 1732, never provided a Blessington heir. With his death, the titles Baron Boyle and Viscount Blessington became extinct, and the estates in Blessington and Monkstown devolved to his sister Anne. When she died in 1741, the estate passed to her son, William Stewart, who on his father's side inherited the Mountjoy estates and the titles of Viscount Mountjoy and Baron Stewart.[41] Four years later Stewart acquired the additional title of Earl of Blessington. But he also inherited the Boyle ill luck with regard to heirs; his only child, a son, predeceased him. When he died in 1769, the Blessington title became extinct once again, and all the Boyle estates – Blessington, Monkstown, county Dublin, and Monkstown, county Cork –3

passed to Charles Dunbar, a grandson of Morough's daughter Mary. The Stewart estate went to a paternal Mountjoy cousin.[42]

Charles Dunbar was MP for Blessington and also represented, for a short period, the borough of Hillsborough. He lived in Dublin at Sackville Street and later at Westland Row, where he and his wife, Penelope, who was described as a woman of charm, beauty and culture and was said to have endowed a school at

Blessington, were prominent members of society.[43] However, in true Boyle tradition, Charles Dunbar died heirless in 1778, but not before he had made a will reiterating the wishes of his great-grandfather, Morough Boyle, that the estate continue 'in the family and blood of the late Primate Boyle'. It was at this stage that the estates in Dublin and Cork were divided among Boyle's descendants. The Blessington estate was inherited by Wills Hill, a descendant from Eleanor Boyle's marriage with William Hill. Wills was the great-great-grandson of Archbishop Boyle, and would later become the first Marquis of Downshire.

Wills Hill also inherited Archbishop Boyle's copy of Bedell's Irish translation of the Old Testament. This was believed to have been a gift to the archbishop from his kinsman, Robert Boyle, the noted scientist, through whose 'goodwill' this first Irish translation of the bible was made.[44] An inscription on the bible (which is now held in the Parish of Hillsborough, county Down), notes that it came into the possession of the Bishop of Dromore, Dr T Percy, who subsequently presented it to Wills Hill.

❧ 3 The Downshire Connection

'By God and the Sword I Obtained Possession.'

HILL FAMILY MOTTO

The family fortunes of the Downshires originated with Moyses Hill, a landless young gentleman from the west country in England, who first came to Ireland in the 1570s in the reign of Elizabeth I. He fought in the unsuccessful campaign of Walter Devereux, the first Earl of Essex, to break the power of Sorley Boy MacDonnell of the Antrim Glens and his ally Turlough O'Neill, and subsequently served under Essex and Mountjoy in the war against Hugh O'Neill, Earl of Tyrone.[1] The first territory he acquired was a grant from the Crown in 1592 for lands in the vicinity of Larne on a lease of twenty-one years. Over the following two centuries this small foothold was enlarged and extended as the Hill family steadily acquired land and titles and established themselves at Hillsborough. By the end of the eighteenth century, their estates extended to over 100,000 statute acres and, except for the acquisition of some small parcels of land in the first half of the nineteenth century, they remained largely unchanged until their dispersal under the Land Acts of the late nineteenth and early twentieth centuries.[2] The militant nature of the family motto *Per Deum et Ferrum Obtinui* – By God and the Sword I Obtained Possession – was modified in later years by the more peaceful practice of forging family alliances.

One of the more notable members of the family was Wills Hill, who married Margaretta Fitzgerald, a sister of the Earl of Kildare, thus, like the Boyles, aligning himself with one

45

of the county's premier Anglo-Norman families. Wills succeeded his father in 1742 and from then until his death some fifty years later was active in the public sphere. He held many positions of note including Secretary of State for the American Colonies. He strongly opposed the colonists' demand for a relaxation in taxes and his stance on the issue eventually forced him to resign. He was even blamed by some for the loss of the colonies. His lack of political acumen led Horace Walpole to describe him as an ambitious man possessing 'more pomp than solidity'. Even George III declared that he 'did not know a man of less judgement than Lord Hillsborough'.[3]

Hill was more successful on the home front and was regarded as an example of an improving landlord. It was under his direction that Banbridge developed as the centre of the linen industry in the north-east of the country and he was responsible for the rebuilding of the castle and town of

31 Linen making in county Down

32 Wills Hill, first Marquis of Downshire

Hillsborough. In his last speech to the Westminster House
of Lords in 1786, Hill argued strongly for a union between
Britain and Ireland as the best method of consolidating the
interests of both kingdoms. Throughout his life he acquired
a string of titles, said to have been equal to the number
bestowed on Wellington and double those awarded to
Nelson, which included Baron Harwich, Viscount Kilwarlin
and Earl of Hillsborough, crowned in 1789 by the
conferring of the marquisate of Downshire. It was during
his lifetime that the Hill family inherited the Blessington
estate in 1778.

By then the ambitious hopes of Archbishop Boyle for
Blessington had not been realised. The town had failed to
expand, the corporation had long since ceased to exist, the
house and demesne were neglected. Wills Hill sought to

remedy this and under a writ granted by George III restored Blessington's corporation. In July 1781, an election to a new corporation was held and John Patrickson, subsequently clerk to the Privy Council in Dublin and a confidant of Wills, became sovereign while Theo Jones and Stephen Wybrant, the 'receiver of rent' or the agent in Blessington, were elected bailiffs. For the occasion, Wills commissioned a ceremonial mace, now held in the Ulster Museum in trust for the Downshire Estate. How long the corporation remained in operation is not known but the last recorded sovereign of the town was in 1796 when John Patrickson's brother, William, held the position. The corporation elected two of its members to sit in the Irish Parliament, but this was 'the merest formality' as the only voters were the burgesses themselves and they were appointed by the 'the Lord of the Manor', namely Downshire himself.[4]

Wills next turned his attention to refurbishing Blessington House as a summer residence for his family. The work was undertaken by the builder and architect, Charles Lilly, who was also employed on Hillsborough Castle and Downpatrick Cathedral. Between 1785 and 1786, as many as twelve men were employed bringing materials from Dublin. Alex Bourke, Pat Dunne, William Sergeant, John Folld, John Mulvey, John Ryan, Farrell Costello, Charles Kelly and Michael Quigley supplied slates, while John Foley and Val Whelan brought 1,300 deal boards each, and William Kelly brought an additional 900. At first much of the work was concentrated on the stables and the demesne and gave employment to a large number of the residents of the town. A variety of tradesmen – a mason, plumber, carpenter, smithy, roofer and glazier as well as hauliers, a stonecutter and bell repairer – were needed. James Ivers repaired the roof, for which he received £4 14s for forty-seven days work, Willim Twyford repaired the coping for which William Tassie supplied the cut stone, and Alex Bourke fitted glass in the stables as well as in the barn and wool room. Twyford also supervised the labourers – Ned Doyle, Con Kelly, Roger Connolly, Ned Doolin, Thady Cagher, Pady Neal and Ned Farrell as well as two men by the names of Quinn and Doran who repaired the demesne wall. Charles Kavanagh received £4 11s for hanging gates on the avenue, while Benjamin Hughes looked after the haggard gates. Edward Kelly, the 'lymeburner', supplied 189 hogsheads of lime for £8 13s and Alex Bourke's horse was hired for three days to remove rubbish. Bourke also carried out the glazing in the upper chapel room, bedchamber, housekeeper's room, pantry and laundry. John Nowlan repaired the bells in the main reception rooms, including the great hall, the big parlour, the drawing and breakfast rooms, as well as various bedchambers. Extensive plumbing work was also undertaken and included installing water closets, while a locksmith, Richard Homan, had the task of securing the house. [5]

In November 1786, William Greene, one of Hill's employees, visited Blessington and sent back a report on the repairs taking place: 'the roof and slating of the stables are extremely well executed and the repair of the park wall [is] going on well and in the cheapest manner'.[6] The general state of the house, however, was a cause for concern especially in view of the inclement weather Greene experienced during his visit. The rain came 'several times in great plenty after every high wind that blew while I was there', and only by 'a weekly expense' to the roof was the rain kept from ruining the mansion. He warned that the roof would not stand another winter. More extensive work continued in the following years and by 1791 redecorating was in progress; '42 dozen sattin ground tabby paper' and a border to match at a cost of almost £12 had been bought and £1 16s was spent on 'twice coulouring the parlour'.[7]

In 1793, Wills Hill, first Marquis of Downshire, died and was succeeded by his son Arthur. By that time, the Hill family were among the wealthiest landowners in Ireland and England. Arthur had married Mary Sandys,

33 Arthur Hill, second Marquis of Downshire

'considered one of the richest of her sex in the empire', with a reputed £60,000 in ready money and £3,000 a year 'besides her expectations'. Her wealth was inherited from both parents. Her father, Martin, a younger son of Baron Sandys of Ombersley, was the only one of seven brothers to leave an heir and on the death of her uncle, the second Baron Sandys, who was said to be immensely rich, she inherited the Sandys fortune. On her mother's side she was the sole heir of both the Trumbull and Blundell estates; her maternal grandmother, a daughter of Viscount Blundell of Blundell Manor in Edenderry, had married William Trumbull of Easthamsted Park in Berkshire. Through these connections Mary Sandys inherited 14,000 acres at Edenderry, another 5,000 acres in Dundrum, county Down, as well as a mansion and some 500 acres at Easthampstead.[8]

Arthur Hill was an extravagant spender, especially where

his family's honour and position in society were at stake. He was active politically even before he inherited the Downshire title and in a parliamentary election in 1790 unsuccessfully tried to secure control of county Down against a challenge from Robert Stewart, the future Viscount Castlereagh. He later admitted to spending £30,000 on that election, as a result of which he had to 'lead a most uncomfortable life for six or eight months'.[9] Despite his wife's wealth, Arthur had difficulties meeting his financial responsibilities, and debts built up against the estate. Hard cash was scarce and shortly after he took control of his estates, creditors were at the door. Charles Lilly, the builder of both Hillsborough Castle and Blessington House, was pressing for the £800 due for work done in Blessington. Two years later he was back again, this time for work on 'public rooms' at Downpatrick, pointing out that up to then he had only received £311 7s 6d, a fraction of the amount owing.[10] A few years later, George Stephenson, one of Downshire's agents in the north, reported to Arthur, then living at Hanover Square in London, that all the Hillsborough servants were due three years wages: 'For God's sake, my Lord, have the goodness to direct Mr Lane to pay me something for the servants … some are really starving'.[11]

The Blessington estate of 10,500 Irish (17,000 statute acres) that Arthur Hill inherited was modest compared with his northern estates. It stretched from the ridge of low hills separating west Wicklow from Kildare to the Wicklow mountains in the east. The more low-lying part was to the west but with the exception of the Liffey valley no part fell below 200 metres; on the fringes of the Wicklow mountains, heights over 300 metres were the norm.[12] Most of the lands lay within the barony of Talbotstown Lower in the north-west of the county (baronies were territorial units which were used for administration and taxation purposes from the sixteenth century onwards and may correspond to the old Irish *tuath* or local kingdom).

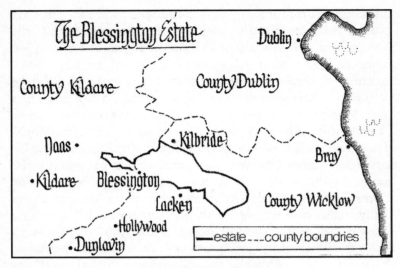

34 The Blessington estate

Of the 36 townlands into which the estate was divided, 31 were in Talbotstown Lower, with the remaining five in the Barony of Naas North in county Kildare.[13] A townland, of which there are 62,000 altogether in Ireland, is the smallest division of land in the country and its origins reflect the various epochs of land settlement in Irish history – Gaelic, Norman, Tudor and Stuart. Although no longer used for any administrative purpose, the townland was important from the seventeenth to the nineteenth centuries in mapping and describing the estates in the country. Size varied greatly, with the bigger townlands usually found in marginal and mountain areas. On the Blessington estate, many of the names of the upland townlands like Ballydonnell, Ballylow, Ballynabrocky, Ballynatona, Ballynasculloge and Ballysmuttan were Gaelic in origin and the inhabitants were mostly Catholic. In contrast, many of the townlands on the better land in areas like Crosscoolharbour, Threecastles, Hempstown, Blackhall and Newtown had English place names. In the eighteenth and nineteenth century these townlands, along with Blessington itself, contained a high proportion of Protestant tenants whose ancestors had most likely been encouraged by Archbishop Boyle to settle on the estate.

An assessment of the quality of the land in the estate can be found in the valuation for the entire country undertaken by Richard Griffith in the mid-nineteenth century.[14] The better land was situated surrounding and to the north of Blessington where the average townland valuation was above 15s an acre but did not exceed £1. This dropped to between 10s and 15s on the Kildare land to the west of the town. In the mountainous area to the east, the drop in valuation was more spectacular with more than half the estate valued as low as 3d an acre. In the uplands, however, tiny pockets of profitable land valued at between 3s and 8s an acre could be found.

During most of the eighteenth century, the country in general was relatively quiet and there was a growth in economic prosperity. The industrial revolution in England brought an increasing demand for Irish agricultural produce and this buoyancy in the market was reflected in

35 The Linen Hall, Dublin

the changing appearance of rural Ireland as the remaining tracts of open land were enclosed with stone walls, ditches and hedges. Dairy farming was thriving, particularly in Munster, a fact that was noted by Arthur Young in his celebrated tour of Ireland in the late 1770s: 'great farmers hire vast quantities of land in order to stock with cows and let them to dairymen; one farmer, who died lately, paid £1,400 a year for this purpose; but 300 or 400 [is] common'.[15] There was also a demand for other Irish products such as glassware, linen, and woollen goods, and in the newly expanding country towns flour-mills and distilleries were built. The road system was improved to facilitate trade and the number of local fairs and markets expanded. In the Blessington area, the general prosperity enabled the larger tenants in Crosscoolharbour, Threecastles and Newtown Great to build themselves comfortable two-storied slated farmhouses.

The eighteenth century saw the planters consolidate the estate system with the building of Georgian mansions surrounded by walled demesnes and parklands planted with trees. Blessington House was not the only big house in the neighbourhood. Four kilometres away was Russborough, a fine example of a neo-classical Palladian mansion, built in the middle of the eighteenth century by Joseph Leeson, the Earl of Milltown. The houses of the minor gentry, such as the Smiths at Baltiboys, the Hornidges at Tulfarris and Russellstown and the Finnemores at Ballyward, were on a more modest scale. Even in the uplands, the landowning class left an impact on the landscape in the form of shooting lodges; the Downshires built a lodge at Ballynabrocky and later at Ballylow in the most remote part of their estate.[16]

ℒ 4 The Rebellion of 1798

'Nothing but anarchy, confusion, plunder and burning.'

REV ROGER MILEY

At the end of the eighteenth century Ireland appeared calm but beneath the veneer of order and ease there was simmering unrest, especially among the Catholics who had been dispossessed of their lands and who had remained on as smallholders under the new ascendancy. The memory of the lands held by their ancestors was kept alive and their dissatisfaction and frustration found expression in agrarian secret societies. The 'Whiteboys', who first made their appearance in county Tipperary in the early 1760s, and others like the 'Houghers', 'Oakboys' and 'Hearts of Steel', were motivated by grievances such as the payment of tithes to a church to which they did not belong, the encroachment of livestock on tillage land and the enclosure of common land. The members were bound by oath and wore disguises like the white shirt worn by the Whiteboys. Local groups worked mainly independently of each other and used public proclamations and letters to threaten individuals whom they felt were oppressing smallholders. Destruction to property or livestock often ensued.

In 1791, the Society of United Irishmen was formed; it was a movement influenced by the revolutionary ideas of the time which saw expression in the American War of Independence and later in the French Revolution. The initial membership was middle-class; in Belfast it was associated with a group of Presbyterians, in Dublin it comprised a mixture of both Protestants and Catholics.

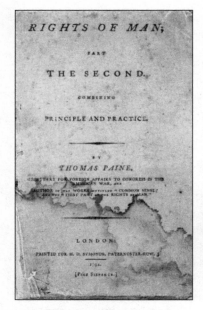

36 *Title page* Rights of Man

37 *An informer*

38 *Army reprisals*

Greatly influenced by Thomas Paine's *Rights of Man*, it aimed to bring about parliamentary reform through the brotherhood of all Irishmen, irrespective of religion. At first a peaceful movement, seeking its objectives through publishing pamphlets, debates and presenting petitions to Parliament, it later became a secret oath-bound society, pledged to establish an Irish republic with French backing. The movement spread quickly, swelled by the numerous small tenants in agrarian secret societies. The members were mostly untrained and armed only with crudely made pikes but many Catholic militiamen secretly joined and were ready to defect to the insurgents when the rising occurred.[1] In December 1796, a French fleet arrived off Bantry Bay in county Cork, but bad weather prevented it from landing. The authorities responded by giving free rein to the military, yeomanry and militia to hunt down the United Irishmen. This resulted in terrible atrocities, and executions, half-hangings, pitch-capping and the firing of homesteads became widespread throughout the country during 1797.

Some years before the rebellion broke out, a direct line of communication had been established between Blessington and Dublin Castle. John Smith, an Englishman who previously had been a member of a Belfast branch of the United Irishmen, and William McCormack, both Castle spies, were based in Blessington, and regularly passed on information about local disturbances and United Irishmen sympathisers to the magistrate and vicar, Rev Hill Benson, and to Downshire's agent, William Patrickson.[2] Hill Benson, who was giving information to Dublin Castle as late as 1803, had most likely Hillsborough connections; in 1773, at the reopening of Hillsborough Church following its restoration under Wills Hills, a Rev Hill Benson had said the prayers while an Archdeacon Benson had preached the sermon. The Patricksons were by now substantial tenants on the Blessington estate. William Patrickson, as the Downshire agent, had supervised improvements to

Blessington House on behalf of the second marquis, and was the tenant of the Demesne and Deerpark. Both he and his brother John held leases on a number of houses and sites in the town in addition to their farms in Oldcourt, and William also had the interest of land in the adjoining parish of Kilbride. John was clerk of the Irish Privy Council in Dublin and a confidant of the second marquis, who now mainly resided in London. He was pivotal in keeping the marquis regularly briefed about his Irish estates and about national affairs.

The first rumblings of disaffection in the Blessington area occurred in 1796 when the local inhabitants refused to bring provisions or supply turf to the troops stationed at Russborough. John Smith put the blame on Joseph and John Leeson, nephews of Lord Milltown, whom he suspected of being supporters of the United Irishmen – a view shared by John Patrickson. In August of the following year, a more serious incident took place. One of the Castle spies, William McCormack, infiltrated the local branch of the United Irishmen and was about to give evidence against them at the county assizes. Determined to prevent this, 'two to three hundred local men rushed into the town brandishing pikes and muskets' and surrounded his house. The local yeomen, headed by Richard Hornidge of Tulfarris and William Patrickson, were unable to protect him; he was dragged from his home and murdered. The same day Hill Benson's house was also attacked and the authorities immediately offered a reward of £100 for information leading to the arrest of those responsible. This reward was supplemented by subscriptions from the local Wicklow gentry; Lords Aldborough, Waterford, Powerscourt and Fitzwilliam all subscribed in the region of £50 while the marquis contributed £113.[3] The failure of the Blessington yeomanry to protect McCormack struck terror into the hearts of other informers in the area, among whom were five Belfast men who had been driven from their homes by United Irishmen and who regarded Blessington

39 Enemy view of United Irishmen in training

as a safe haven. John Smith particularly became alarmed for his own safety but history, unfortunately, does not tell us how his story ended.

Throughout the winter of 1797 tension in the town increased. Reports of an imminent rising in the country persisted and in March 1798, John Patrickson reported to the marquis that Wicklow county was 'in a wretched state' of lawlessness. The following month William Patrickson was warned that 'a party of between sixty and a hundred of these deluded people' planned to murder him, and so his brother John asked Downshire for permission to convert the inn in Blessington to accommodate the cavalry. In early May, John reported that Blessington House had been raided a few nights previously and seven guns, two cases of pistols and three swords taken. The same night John Finnemore's home at Ballyward had been attacked but after a 'great length of firing' Finnemore felt his safest option was to give the rebels what they were looking for and threw out his guns to them. Arms were also seized that night from thirteen local yeomen.[4]

40 Repulsing a rebel attack

The long-expected rebellion finally broke out on the night of 23 May in counties Kildare and Meath, followed by Wexford some days later. One of the first engagements took place at Naas, less than fifteen kilometres from Blessington. An estimated 3,000 insurgents attacked the garrison four times but although they fought bravely they were no match for the regular army. One hundred and sixty-two were reported killed and the many who were taken prisoner were 'immediately hanged in the streets'.[5] Kilcullen and Ballymore Eustace also saw action the same day but the rebels were easily defeated. Those who escaped dispersed to the nearby Wicklow hills where they formed a camp at Blackamore Hill close to Blessington.

A week later Blessington itself came under attack. John Patrickson reported to the marquis that 'Blessington House and all its appendage and everything appertaining ... are completely destroyed' and houses belonging to his brother William were burnt, leaving him 'ruined as to his fortune'.[6] Days later, the rebels returned to complete the destruction of the town. They 'burned or destroyed every good house in

41 Sacking a landlord's house

it' except the Post Office and a house belonging to Mrs
Farley, a sister of Roger Miley, the parish priest of nearby
Crosschapel.[7] Harsh retaliatory action was taken by the
army and yeomanry who in turn burnt the houses of anyone
suspected of being a rebel.[8]

The attack on Blessington was denounced not only by
the loyalists; Catholics were equally horrified by what they
had witnessed. In June, Rev Miley wrote to Dr Troy, the
Catholic Archbishop of Dublin, describing what had
happened: 'For some days past we are totally convulsed
both here and in the neighbouring parishes: every moral
and religious sentiment has quit the country ... nothing but
anarchy, confusion, plunder and burning ... the Marquis of
Downshire's fine edifice at Blessinton with its offices are
razed, all the fine furniture of every kind carried away ... the
cottages of the poor and the ... middling class have shared
the same fate'. Miley was so upset by what he saw that he
'was just upon the point of flying to town' when concern for
his 'once beloved but now deluded and unfortunate people'
prevented him from abandoning them. What he described

as his 'feeble exertions to support peace and order in my parish and neighbourhood', earned him the public praise and thanks of the army commanders.[9]

In September the town experienced yet another attack from the rebels holding out in the hills beyond Blessington. They remained in the town for some days and from there made raids on neighbouring farms, seizing 400 cattle and 150 sheep; the taking of such a large number of animals had probably as much to do with reprisals as it did with the need to find provisions. Once again the local yeomanry, who barricaded themselves in St Mary's Church, were totally ineffectual and Hill Benson was forced to protect his own home.[10] In Ballyward, John Finnemore, according to his own account, was taken by force to Blackamore Hill on the orders of one of the rebel leaders, General Reynolds; he was kept in the rebel camp from a Monday until the following Thursday, when in his own words 'he got away from them'.[11]

Although the rebellion in the country at large was over by 1798, Blessington remained in a state of lawlessness. John Patrickson cited the case of 'one of our poor Protestant neighbours near the Horseshoe' who had been 'taken out of his bed and shot' because he was suspected of carrying information to William Patrickson.[12] In his eyes, it was a grim warning: 'No day, no night, passes without numerous robberies, murders and burnings ... if something is not shortly done there will not be a Protestant left in our part of the country. The Papists are entirely in possession, for all those who have not been killed are banished'. This made him fear that the Downshire estate would 'suffer to a great degree' because so many tenants had left. Among those tenants were Anne Browne of Walshestown who was burnt out of her house and forced to take refuge with her large family in Dublin, and Richard Austin and his family in Haylands who disappeared without trace following the rebellion. John Smith, brother-in-law of Elizabeth, was forced to emigrate to Paris after the burning of Baltiboys

House during the rebellion, and John Patrickson himself eventually left for London, never to return.

Blessington was now in ruins and the countryside about devastated. 'There is hardly a tree left standing', except at Russborough where 'all ... is perfect', an escape Patrickson attributed to John Leeson's sympathies for the United Irishmen.[13] But gradually life returned to normal and people began assessing the damage to their property. A Government commission was established almost immediately to consider the claims of the 'suffering loyalists'. In the Blessington area, many people submitted claims but Downshire's – in excess of £10,000 for the destruction of his house and property – was by far the largest. The most common claim related to crops and animals but compensation for damage to houses, household effects and even apparel was sought. Dr Edward Parsley sought compensation for damage to 'medical and electrical apparatus', and Henry and William Norton for looms and weaving apparatus.[14] John Finnemore claimed for a long list of disasters that befell him during the rebellion. Not alone was his house burnt but his farm was left almost

42 *Part of John Finnemore's letter of claim*

bereft of animals; 73 bullocks, 12 cows, upwards of 50 veal calves and all his sheep and lambs were stolen, as well as meal, potatoes, bacon and two carcasses of beef for the use of his family and servants. In addition, bank notes to the value of £900 hidden in an outbuilding and £600 in cash secreted in various parts of the house had disappeared. Much of the cash was later found in the possession of one of his servant-girls, who was apprehended while fleeing to Dublin, and although Finnemore had suspicions about the identity of the thief who had taken the £900 in notes, he did nothing about it as 'the boy's relations lived about him up in the mountains'.[15]

Catholics who sought reimbursement included the parish priest, Roger Miley, whose house was damaged and who had horses and sheep stolen from his farm, Rose Brady from Ballysmuttan who lost a horse and bedding, and Henry Cassidy of Blackrock whose house was damaged. During the four years it sat, the commission distributed over one million pounds. The marquis received £9,000, John Finnemore and William Patrickson each got in excess of £2,000, while Charles Lilly, the builder, and William Tassie, one of the larger farmers in Threecastles, both received more than £600. In nearby Russellstown, Cuthbert Hornidge was awarded over £4,000. Not all the claimants were successful and it is unclear how many people suffered the fate of Charles Bryan of Kilbride who sought £25 for damage to his orchard and the loss of profits from his cows only to be turned down.[16]

The most significant consequence of the Rebellion was the determination of the British Government, alarmed by the support the rebels had received from France, to force a union between England and Ireland. The Irish parliament in Dublin was abolished and direct rule from Westminster followed. Bribery in one form or another was used to entice members of parliament to vote themselves out of office and the bill was passed without 'the protesting echo of a sigh'.[17] Many, like the second marquis, were against the Union. But he paid heavily for his opposition. He lost all his official positions in Ireland – Colonel of the Downshire militia, Governor of county Down, member of the Irish Privy Council and holder of a sinecure in the Court of Chancery. His wife believed all of these losses contributed towards his early death.

43 Title page of Act of Union

Arthur, second Marquis of Downshire, died in Hillsborough on 7 September 1801 and his widow, Mary Sandys, ran the estate on behalf of her eldest son, also called Arthur, who was then only thirteen years of age. She believed that women were as capable in business as men and a special Act of Parliament, which also created her Baroness Sandys of Ombersley in her own right, gave her the authority to participate in all aspects of the running of the estate, including the granting of leases.[18] It was not an easy stewardship. A month after her husband's death, a Dublin attorney, John Pollock, wrote to John Reilly, an administrator in the Downshire accounts office, that the Downshire family finances were in 'general confusion' and that 'the numerous creditors are becoming outrageous for their interest'.[19] The debts incurred by the first and second marquis could no longer be ignored and Mary Sandys had to use part of her own inheritance to pay the most pressing of these. She also had to call on the £55,000 given by the government around this time in compensation for the parliamentary boroughs lost by the family as a result of the Act of Union.[20]

Despite all these troubles, the baroness found time for a busy social life. She was part of the court circle and friendly with the Prince of Wales, the future George IV. She was present at a dinner party at Brighton Pavilion in 1805, when the Prince 'in a merry mood' used an air-gun to shoot at a target placed at the end of the dining room. He invited the ladies to do likewise but all declined except the baroness who missed the target and hit one of the fiddlers providing the music for the evening. On the political level, she actively campaigned to keep up the family's position in the north and granted upwards of 1,000 leases thus increasing the number of '40-shilling freeholders' or those who had the right to vote.[21] She made such an impact on her political opponents that one of them ruefully remarked that 'the appearance of this cursed woman in this county hath excited as much emotion as that of Maria Teresa in Hungary'.[22]

Mary Sandys continued to have an interest in the estate, even after handing over the reins to her son. When the widow of a Kilwarlin tenant on the Hillsborough estate was about to lose her holding following the expiration of the lease after her husband's death, Mary Sandys successfully intervened with the administration, arguing that the widow was well able to run the holding in trust for her young sons.

In 1809, Arthur, the third marquis, came of age and the care of the Downshire estates was in his hands until the middle of the nineteenth century.

5 Bad Debts and Good Neighbours

'Not a bad landlord if he would be quiet about it.'

ELIZABETH SMITH

The coming of age of Arthur Blundell Sandys Trumbull Hill was celebrated in all parts of the estate.[1] From Blessington his agent, Hill Benson, reported that the bonfires 'on every hill and illumination in the very huts' were such that 'dark as the night was, any person might have travelled through any part of the estate commodiously'.[2] But behind the splendour of titles, estates and great houses lay sombre reality. The third marquis had inherited an enormous debt of £300,000, which he spent the remainder of his life attempting to reduce.

Landed families in those days might have had large incomes but they often had equally large claims on their property. By far the most crippling were the legal settlements on various family members such as dowagers and younger sons and daughters. Sizeable parts of estates had to be mortgaged to finance these settlements, and so loans accumulated from one generation to the next. These burdens intensified if widows survived for any great length of time. Although not all outlived their husbands by over fifty years, as did Penelope Dunbar and the first Countess of Milltown, the wives of many Irish peers in the 1780s could look forward to a widowhood of an average of twenty-one years.[3] Wakefield, a prominent social observer of the time, maintained that many landowners in Ireland had not a shilling to their name due to legal settlements.[4] This situation was aptly summed up by a character in a novel of

67

the day who declared that his estate was so tied up that he wished he had 'never had any ancestors'.[5]

The Downshires were particularly burdened by family settlements and from the middle of the eighteenth century onwards the estate was increasingly tied up by mortgages and loans. When Wills Hill inherited the Blessington estate in 1778, it was encumbered by an annuity of £2,000, which had been fixed for life by the previous owner, Charles Dunbar, on his wife Penelope. Although she later married an Englishman, Joshua Iremonger, the annuity continued to be paid out of the Blessington rents until she died in 1829. On the occasion of the marriage of Wills Hill to Lady Margaretta Fitzgerald in 1747, a sum of £10,000 had been settled on each younger child of the marriage, and £2,000 per annum on Lady Margaretta herself in the event of her widowhood. As security for this settlement, most of the estates in county Down and in Carrickfergus were mortgaged. But in this case Lady Margaretta predeceased her husband and the estate was saved the burden of this settlement but a loan of £20,000 had still to be raised for the two daughters of the marriage and this remained a burden on the estate throughout the nineteenth century. The second marquis made a settlement on his wife Mary Sandys, who would receive £5,000 annually after his death, and he also made provision for the younger children of the marriage as follows: £20,000 for one child, £30,000 for two, and £40,000 for three or more. Mary Sandys survived her husband by thirty-five years and until her death in 1836 two-thirds of the rental income from the Dundrum and Edenderry estates went to pay her settlement. The third marquis made similar provisions for his wife Maria, daughter of the Earl of Plymouth, and their children.[6]

Despite their debts, the Downshires like other landed families of the time maintained estates and large houses, had an expensive payroll of officials and numerous servants, and, especially if they moved in court circles, felt obliged to uphold their position in society. Among their various

44 Carton

financial commitments, the upkeep of the family home or 'big house' was one of the most burdensome. Carton, home of the Duke of Leinster, brother-in-law of the first Marquis of Downshire, was described as the centre of an enterprise more 'industrial than domestic'. Over a hundred servants, indoor and outdoor, were employed and the house and out-offices contained an assortment of kitchens, ice-houses, wash-houses, coal sheds, stables, potting-sheds and hothouses, as well as a bakehouse, brewery, tannery, and granary. When guests came to stay, which was frequently, they brought with them their own personal servants – maids, hairdressers and valets – all of whom could double the number of domestic staff to be housed and fed.[7] When Wills Hill inherited Blessington House, the family already possessed two other residences – Hillsborough Castle in county Down and a town house in Hanover Square, London. Later, with the marriage of his son Arthur to Mary Sandys, Easthamstead Park in Berkshire, which the family subsequently used as their main residence, was added to the list.

Landed families saw it as part of their way of life to travel extensively and often lived in Europe for several months a year. The Grand Tour, an extended visit to Europe lasting a number of years, was considered an essential part of the education of sons. Accompanied by their tutors, they attended formal education classes in various European cities and took the opportunity to invest in furnishings and antiques from the classical world – the first and second earls of Milltown were notable in this regard. William Fitzgerald, the eldest son of the Duke of Leinster, travelled extensively in France, Italy, Germany and Switzerland in the 1760s. While in Rome, which was considered the epicentre of the Grand Tour, he studied mathematics as well as dancing. In Florence, he attended *conversazione* classes, bought vases and copies of old masters to adorn Carton, and amused himself with his contemporaries from Eton who were in the city at the time. He returned home 'physically and financially exhausted' after three years of travel. But travel was not only confined to elder sons. Caroline Fox, a sister of the Duchess of Leinster, spent many winters in the 1760s travelling with her family in France, Italy and Belgium. In between 'bouts of hectic spending', the family filled their time socialising with their European counterparts and taking the waters at fashionable spas where the men made 'distant and humble love' to pretty women and the ladies 'gambled with the gentlemen'.[8]

There were other demands on the finances of landed families. Many social services, which today are provided by the state, were in the eighteenth and nineteenth centuries dependent on the goodwill of the gentry. The Downshires, like many of their peers, endowed schools and churches, contributed to mendicity societies and supplied food and clothing to the needy, especially in times of distress. They invested in agricultural improvements on their estates and developed towns like Hillsborough and Dundrum in the north and Blessington and Edenderry in the south. The first Marquis of Downshire was active at the court of George III and held positions in government but after the second marquis's bruising experience in opposing the Act of Union, the family was never again prominent in public life.

The absentee landlord is a recurring theme in Irish history but it was a phenomenon not peculiar to Ireland. Louis XIV insisted that French landowners live in Versailles rather than on their estates but in Ireland the consequences of absenteeism were very great. Already in the eighteenth century the social life of many Irish landed families mainly centred on London, the capital of an expanding empire, which offered good marriage opportunities for sons and daughters, and the passing of the Act of Union in 1800 strengthened this trend. The Union necessitated the presence in London of members of parliament, and Dublin, which had experienced an upsurge in confidence and growth especially in the previous half century, declined.

45 Dublin after the Union

The Downshire neighbours in the Blessington area were mainly non-resident. Some, like Downshire himself, had large estates elsewhere in Ireland and England. Burgage

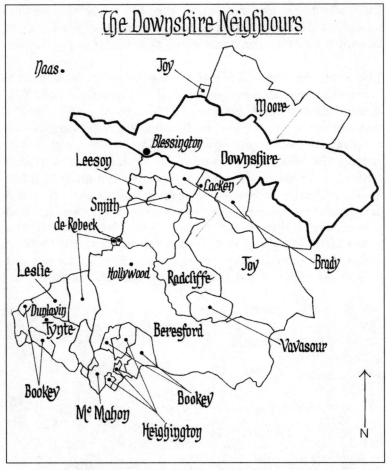

46 The Downshire neighbours in Talbotstown Lower

with its adjoining townlands was the property of the Protestant See of Dublin (it is estimated that a quarter of Irish land was owned by the Church of Ireland). The Marquis of Waterford, Lord Beresford, who owned 15,000 acres centred on the old medieval manor of Hollywood south of Blessington, had estates in both Waterford and England. The Joy family, who held 11,000 acres extending from Lacken to Glenbride, owned much of the Malone area of Belfast, while the de Robeck family, who owned 4,500 acres ten kilometres south of Blessington, had land elsewhere in Wicklow, in Kildare and county Dublin.[9] Many of the smaller landlords in the area were also non-resident; the Bradys lived in Clare, the Bookeys at Derrybawn House in the east of the county, while the Vavasours had a London address. To compound the problem, most of these estates had non-resident agents. Lord Beresford's agent, George Mara, lived in Waterford, George Joy from Belfast managed Lady Joy's Wicklow estate, the Vavasour land was looked after by John Jones of Baltinglass, while a Mr Ebbs of Rathmore in nearby Kildare was agent for the Brady lands. Beyond the collection of rents, these landlords and their agents took little interest in the estate or the tenants.[10]

The de Robecks at least had a resident agent, James Lynch of Whitleas near Ballymore Eustace, who was their principal tenant; by the 1870s the family had settled on the estate at Gowran Grange in Swordlestown not far from Naas, where they farmed the demesne land and personally managed the estate. The Kilbride estate was leased at the beginning of the nineteenth century by George Ponsonby, who was Lord Chancellor of Ireland for a brief period in 1806, and held land throughout the country.[11] He was a liberal and a noted lawyer who acted as counsel for both Henry Sheares and Oliver Bond, leaders of the Dublin directory of the United Irishmen, and although non-resident, he took an active interest in his Kilbride holding and was personally known to both his own tenants and many of those on the neighbouring Downshire estate. In the 1830s the Kilbride estate was acquired by the Moore family who built a manor house and took up residence there; Ogle Moore was not only the local landlord but also the rector of both St Mary's Church in Blessington and St John's at Cloughleagh, the newly built church on his estate.

Of the Downshire neighbours who were resident, the

most aristocratic were the Leesons who lived at Russborough. The family was descended from Hugh Leeson, who came from Culworth in Northhamptonshire in the latter part of the seventeenth century and quickly established a successful brewery on the south side of St Stephen's Green in Dublin, where he also had a 'fashionable house' with extensive gardens. His son Joseph, expanded into property and bought several houses in the city; Dean Swift said of him that he was a 'fanatic brewer, [and was] reported to have some hundreds of houses in this town'.[12] His son, also called Joseph, accumulated several titles and eventually became Earl of Milltown. In addition to building a new town house on the north side of Stephen's Green, he acquired a sizeable estate of some 4,000 acres in Drehid and Parsonstown near Carbury, as well as Russellstown and Kilmalum adjoining Blessington. In 1741 he commenced work on Russborough, where the family lived until the beginning of the twentieth century. Among the minor gentry in the area were the Hornidges of Tulfarris and Russellstown, the Finnemores of Ballyward near Kilbride and the Smiths of Baltiboys. Although they lived in less splendour than the Milltowns or Downshires, they were nonetheless a privileged class, especially in the eyes of the ordinary tenants.

The first Hornidge in Ireland was James, a Cromwellian soldier who received a grant of land in Colemanna in county Carlow towards the end of the 1650s. By the 1740s the family was well established at Tulfarris and in addition rented land in parts of Kildare where they became large graziers. Forty years later Major Richard Hornidge was active in local government as county sheriff; he was in charge of the local yeomen in 1798. The Hornidges continued to live in Tulfarris until the 1950s. Another branch of the family leased land in nearby Russellstown from the Earl of Milltown.

The Finnemores were among the earliest recorded tenants, leasing land from Morough Boyle, the first

47 *Russborough*

Viscount Blessington, in 1700, and they also held land in the adjoining parish of Kilbride.[13] They were related to the Patricksons and like the Hornidges were large graziers; they lived at Ballyward House until the beginning of the twentieth century. Astute and careful with their money, they were in a position to lend to both the third marquis and his father before him.

The most colourful of the Downshire neighbours was Elizabeth Smith who lived at Baltiboys House on a small estate of 1,200-acres in the townland of Baltiboys Lower, three kilometers from Blessington. Elizabeth, born in Edinburgh in May 1797, belonged to a very old Gaelic Scottish clan, the Grants of Rothiemurchus, and spent her summers in the Highlands, where her father, the seventh laird, had inherited a family house. Their fortunes always verged on bankruptcy, due as much to her father trying 'to keep up the traditional style in which neighbours and tenants expected him to live' as to his personal ambition. In an effort to improve the family finances, he read law in London but the expense of setting up chambers and a family home in Lincoln's Inn only added to his burdens. When he lost his seat in Parliament in 1827, he was

48 Henry Smith   *49 Elizabeth Smith*

deprived of whatever protection he had from his debtors and was forced to flee to France and from there to India, where through family influence he was appointed a judge. Throughout this time Elizabeth and her sister Jane earned money by writing articles for Scottish magazines, which enabled them and their mother to survive and eventually journey to India to be reunited with their father.[14] Elizabeth always had a literary turn of mind; she acted as her father's legal and personal secretary and catalogued his library 'rather slowly because she could not stop herself reading the books'.[15]

In India, Elizabeth met and married Colonel Henry Smith, an army officer in the employment of the East India Company. But she was not to live out her life in India. The Smiths were an established west Wicklow family and various members served as county sheriffs in Wicklow in the eighteenth century. Henry and his older brother John were members of the yeomanry in 1798 but when John moved to Paris after the rebellion the estate was neglected. On his death Henry inherited and he and Elizabeth returned.

On her arrival in Ireland Elizabeth threw all her skill and energies into the management of the estate, partly because of her husband's lack of involvement which may have arisen from ill-health; he suffered from frequent bouts of asthma. The colonel or Hal, as she called him, had a debonair approach to life and was the stereotypical Irish landowner of the time as depicted in Maria Edgeworth's *Castle Rackrent* – restless, convivial and with a passion for horses. Although he had the final say on the larger policy issues relating to the estate, it was Elizabeth who managed things on a day-to-day basis. She was particularly active in introducing new agricultural practices and her involvement in the running of the estate was probably unique for her time. Her experience as a member of the Grant clan coloured her view of the relationship which, she believed, ought to exist between landowner and tenant – a view which was not always shared by the tenants at Baltiboys. She believed that the Scottish system, where the head of the clan knew all his dependants by name and where 'their well-being [was] as much his object as that of his own family', was the answer to many of the ills in Irish society. Distressed that no such relationship existed between the Baltiboys tenants and their landlord, she was determined to do all she could to foster an affectionate but paternalistic relationship with them. 'There was nothing struck me so remarkably when I first came here as the tenants marrying their children – setting them up in different trades, etc. without ever saying one word about it to their landlord. It went through their whole conduct – we were to them only the receivers of a much grudged rent'.[16]

Elizabeth kept a diary from the 1840s to her death in 1885 in which she recorded the details of her daily life. She had considerable literary ability and her acerbic wit captured the foibles of both the neighbouring Blessington gentry and her tenants. Though she was not the social equal of the Downshires or the Milltowns she was in no doubt about her rightful place in society. As the Leesons' wealth was based not on land and rent-rolls but on trade this brought out the streak of snobbishness in her. When the Earl of Milltown's fondness for gambling brought the family into financial difficulties, she wondered at his wife's exalted opinion of herself and felt that the earl's peerage, 'bought in Mr Pitt's time by a Brewer', was hardly something to be 'puffed up with pride' about. Lady Milltown was not the only neighbour on whom she sharpened her pen. When, in 1841, Mrs Hornidge and Mrs Finnemore visited her at Baltiboys, she was highly critical. They were 'most beautifully dressed, had they been six-and-thirty and going to a publick breakfast, painted and made up and falsified in every way, they would have looked very well on the stage by lamplight'. Ogle Moore was another who incurred her displeasure. Always conscious of her own long line of descent, she declared of the Moore family that they had 'just four ancestors they can name on the father's side and zero on that score on the mother's'.[17]

Her opinion of the third marquis was coloured by her first experience of him. On his visits to Blessington he stayed at the agent's house in the town and did not socialise much with anyone. Elizabeth was quick to notice this incivility; when the Smiths initially took up residence in the early 1830s, the marquis was the only neighbour who did not call on them although 'the Colonel waited upon him'. Thereafter the Smiths made no attempt to call on Downshire or his wife when they visited Blessington. She considered Downshire a pompous man who had the 'airs of grandeur which perhaps suited the style of the world in the days of his youth', and summed him up in one perceptive sentence: 'Not a bad landlord if he would be quiet about it, though a hard one, nor an unkind master but so full of himself he considers no one else and requiring a degree of subserviency in all his dependants.'[18]

ᕲ 6 Land Tenure and Agents

*'The landlords were sometimes decent men
but the agents were devils one and all.'*

CONTEMPORARY VERDICT

Landholding in Ireland was never just a simple two-tiered
system of landlord and tenant; it was complex and multi-
layered, a product of the day and age.

In the eighteenth century many parts of Ireland were
underpopulated with little investment in agriculture so a
convenient way of managing large estates, especially
prevalent among absentee landowners, was to divide the
land into tracts of 100 to 1,000 Irish acres or more and let
it at a low rent to well-established people who, it was hoped,
would develop the property. These leaseholders would
usually sublet some, if not all, of this land and it was from
them that many tenants held their holdings, rather than
directly from the landowner. In time they became known as
'middlemen'.

The term 'middleman' has traditionally been a pejorative
one but middlemen were not necessarily idle drones. Many
lived on the land they leased and sublet only part; they
became the equivalent of an agricultural middle class,
building large houses, farming the land and in the eyes of
their undertenants performing all the functions of the
landowner at local level. But when they were not resident
and had sublet all their land, the faults of the system soon
emerged. The land tended to be further sublet and
subdivided and the result was a multiplicity of smallholders
living at subsistence level. A notable example of this
occurred on Valentia Island off the Kerry coast where the

local landlord estimated that in fifty years subdivision of holdings had resulted in an increase in the number of tenants from four hundred to over three thousand.[1]

On the Blessington estate in the beginning of the nineteenth century the land held by absentee middlemen was ten per cent (1,700 acres out of a total of 17,000), sublet in holdings of between 110 and 285 acres, mainly in the townlands of Oldcourt, Hempstown, Knockieran, Butterhill and Dillonsdown. Only one of the four leaseholders of Oldcourt, Charles Walsh, was living on his farm; the other three, William and John Patrickson and Charles Lilly, never lived in Oldcourt and when their leases expired towards the middle of the nineteenth century the townland was a typical reflection of the middleman system, with many landless cottiers and smallholders living in poor conditions on tiny acreages.[2]

By far the largest resident holders of land on the estate were the Finnemores. The family lived and worked the land at Ballyward but they also held leases on the upland townlands of Ballylow, Ballydonnell, Ballynasculloge and

50 Ballyward House

Ballynatona, which they in turn sublet to undertenants. Thus they were both tenants of the Downshires and landlords of the tenants to whom they sublet, reflecting both sides of the middleman coin. When John Finnemore died his tenants at Ballylow recorded their high regard for a landlord who had always shown 'paternal solicitude' for their welfare, 'alleviating their miseries by the most cordial acts of benevolence' and collecting their rent in 'small instalments and at such remote periods' as was convenient. When the Finnemore lease expired and Ballylow came directly under the rule of the Downshires this changed and the tenants felt their new landlord never showed them the same sympathy.[3]

Other Finnemore tenants were less enthusiastic. James Murphy, an undertenant in nearby Ballynatona, described his landlord as 'the greatest land huxter that the country could produce'. Murphy paid about £90 a year for his land but Finnemore paid only £22 10s a year to Downshire.[4] This was an anomaly thrown up by the land tenure system. Landowners usually granted long leases in order to ensure stability and encourage investment in the holding. In times of economic boom this worked to their disadvantage as their rents were fixed by the terms of tenure, whereas leaseholders who sublet were more likely to grant shorter leases and could renew them at higher rents.

In the eighteenth and nineteenth century, leases were the exception, not the rule. In general, tenants in the north-eastern counties were more likely to enjoy a formal contract with their landlord than were tenants in the rest of the country. But there was considerable variation. Baron de Robeck granted leases on small as well as large holdings on his estate near Dunlavin, while Lord Beresford granted none at all on his 15,000 acre estate at Hollywood.[5] On the Blessington estate at the end of the eighteenth century, a few key tenants, like the Finnemores and the larger tenants to whom the Downshires let directly, were given leases. It was left to them to decide whether to grant leases to those

51   *The Finnemore lease to Ballylow tenants, 1782*

to whom they sublet. The Finnemores were among those who did. In 1782, a 21-year lease on Ballylow was granted to Laurence Kearny, John Fitzsimons, Peter Murphy, Peter Moran, John Sheridan, Michael Lawler, Matthew Lynch and William Brady at an annual rent of £72.[6]

Early Downshire leases were hand-written on parchment and stipulated the location and size of the holding, the half-yearly rent and the date of payment. Rents were payable half yearly, in May and November, on 'gale' days; generally the tenants were half a year behind in paying rents and this was known as the 'hanging gale'. The term of tenancy was also an important consideration and was fixed either for a specified number of years or for the lives of named people, usually children, or for a combination of both. A lease might be for one, two or three lives and a period of years and expired either on the death of the last surviving named person or after the stipulated period of years, whichever was the longest. On the northern estates of the Downshires many leases granted in the 1700s were for thirty-one years and three lives, which meant that the land could be legally tied up for more than sixty years. A form of lease unknown in England but not uncommon in Ireland was one renewable forever (in the early 1830s, the third marquis successfully got a reversal of such a lease granted in 1679 to Isaac Eccles). There was an important distinction between lives and years; leases for lives were freehold, leases for years were not. Until the end of the eighteenth century, only Protestant freeholders worth at least 40s per annum (40-shilling freeholders) could vote. It was not until 1793 that the Catholic Relief Act extended similar voting rights to Catholic 40-shilling freeholders.[7] There was often a political aspect to granting leases, as when Mary Sandys granted 1,000 leases for one life on the northern estates between 1805-7, thus creating 1,000 extra voters.

Shorter leases of 21 years had always been the norm on the marginal upland areas of the country. These were often held in partnership by a group of tenants, with a head tenant dealing directly with the landowner or middleman (as in the Finnemore lease at Ballylow).

The leases usually contained a number of conditions or covenants. The landowner reserved the rights to game, timber and minerals and he or his agent could enter the holding at all times and seize animals or produce for the non-payment of rent. A dwelling-house, stable and barn, all of specified dimensions, were to be built within three years, and an orchard was to be enclosed, planted and maintained

52 *An estate lease*

in good order.[8] William Patrickson's lease on a 250-acre holding in Oldcourt in 1791 required him to build a house 40 feet long, 20 feet wide and 12 feet high, a stable and barn each 20 feet by 14 feet, to enclose an orchard of one acre with thorn trees, and to plant an oak, ash, elm or alder tree on every perch on the perimeter of his holding. The tenant was also obliged to use a mill named by the landlord. Subletting and the building of other houses or cabins were expressly prohibited.

Covenants were also to be found in the leases that middlemen granted. In the Finnemore lease for Ballylow, in addition to the rent, the subtenants were expected to send 'during the said term four men in every year (whenever he … shall demand the same) to work for him' or 'in lieu thereof shall pay the sum of 8d for each man, and likewise one horse from each in every year or pay the sum of 1s and 6d each in lieu thereof – to be paid as rent'.[9]

It is debatable to what extent any of these covenants were or could have been enforced.[10] The Hillsborough administration seems to have taken an ambivalent attitude to the question; when an agent expressed concern that the tenants were reneging on their covenants, he got the noncommital reply to 'do as he sees fit to prevent this happening'.[11]

The first concern of the third marquis when he came into his inheritance in 1809 was to settle the more pressing debts left behind by his father and grandfather. As a start he mortgaged part of the Castlereagh and Kilwarlin estates in county Down. This raised almost £100,000 but it was nowhere near the amount needed to put the finances of the estate on a firm footing. Not alone had his father mismanaged his private affairs, he had neglected the general running of the estate. Agents were unsupervised, leading to delays and irregularities in the collection and forwarding of rents.[12] In time he would tackle this problem but as his immediate aim was ready cash he embarked on a plan

53 Arthur Hill, third Marquis of Downshire

suggested by Thomas Handley, the family lawyer, to offer some of the tenants in Kilwarlin and Castlereagh longer leases in return for a 'fine' or a sum of money. Many of these tenants had been granted 21-year leases by his mother some years previously but Handley and the chief agent in the north, Major George Matthews, believed that they would be prepared to pay upwards of £10 an acre for leases of two lives and thirty-one years. As the scheme would involve 750 tenants, each with an average of seven acres, a sum in excess of £50,000 might be realised. If successful, the plan would be extended to tenants elsewhere on the estate.

The marquis personally drafted a letter to the tenants explaining his straitened circumstances and appealed to their honour and goodwill. He also warned the tenants that

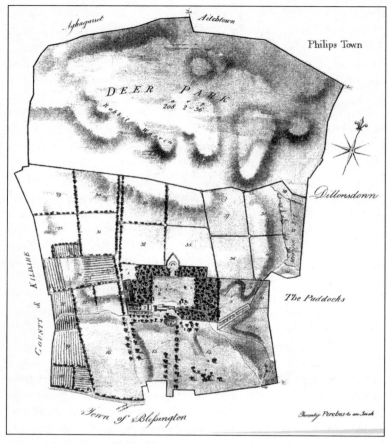

54 Map of Blessington Demesne and Deerpark, 1804

if they did not agree to the deal they might not expect to have their leases renewed at the current rent. The letter, however, was never used. The agent, Matthews, had second thoughts. 'The tenants are extremely cunning,' he warned, and as for appealing to their honour and feeling, 'you might as well think of finding either ... in a Downpatrick potwalloper'. So the scheme was dropped.[13]

The third marquis had made a fumbling start to his administration but it taught him a useful lesson. He decided that from now on the best way to bring his finances under control was to cut back his personal expenditure and to run the estate more efficiently. Concerning his own life style, he decided to live in lodgings while in London rather than at his house in Hanover Square, thus saving £1,000 per annum. He was constantly short of ready cash and on one occasion felt 'cramped to that degree' that he and his family did not move from home except for a ten-day visit to Lord Combermere (whose daughter his son would later marry), and was even 'obliged to ask my mother to lend me £300'. He found this situation irksome. 'It is what I ought not to be compelled to do,' he complained, and declared that his 'means must be more husbanded' so that he might 'have a guinea in my pocket.' Yet he felt the need to meet the expectations of his growing family – 'looking to Lord Hillsborough showing himself a little and Lady Charlotte coming out' – all of which put additional strains on his finances.[14]

Regarding the efficient running of the estate, a start had already been made during his minority. Thomas Handley had been appointed legal adviser and auditor for the entire Downshire estates in England and Ireland, a firm of surveyors undertook a systematic survey and revaluation of the land, and two Scottish engineers, John and Daniel Bushy, were employed to make a mineral survey. But the most immediate problem was rent collection. Up to this the way the rents were collected and accounted for was generally considered to be the agent's own business and consequently the information available to the landlord varied from one part of the estate to another. From now on agents were provided with an official set of books and given instructions on how they were to be kept. These included a rental to be returned to Hillsborough every half year, which contained details of the size, location and occupant of each holding and the amount of the half-yearly rent and arrears when they occurred. A space in it allowed the agent to comment on why arrears arose as well as to detail the measures taken to recoup them. Each agent was also given a ledger, a receipt book to register the rents received and sums paid out, a minute-book for recording the decisions and actions taken concerning the estate, a cash-book and a lease book. The agent's pay was five per cent of the monies collected.[15]

Supervision of the agents was also seen as important. It was decided that Handley, who was based in England, was too remote to oversee the detailed running of the Irish estates, so de Bar, an official from his office, was sent as chief accountant to Hillsborough. Two assistant clerks, Francis Farrah and Joseph Charlesworth, were also employed and henceforth local agents would answer to a head agent and various other officials based in the central office at Hillsborough.

The use of an agent when landowners were non-resident on their estates was commonplace in Ireland in the nineteenth century – even resident landowners such as the Smiths of Baltiboys used an agent. A person of standing in the local area was preferred as he could fulfil some of the social obligations of his landlord as well as being eligible to represent him on the Grand Jury thus furthering the landlord's interest at local level.[16] A professional knowledge of estate management was not necessarily a requirement for the position as it was presumed that a man of the right sort could pick up what he needed to know in the course of doing the job. Neighbouring smaller landowners, junior members of the gentry, retired army officers, lawyers, surveyors, even vicars, were all options.

The Downshire chief agent, who was based at Hillsborough and combined the management of the northern estate with a supervisory role for all the land in Ireland, was usually of high social standing. George Matthews (1800-1813) and William Reilly (1818-1845) were people of some consequence. Matthews, a retired army major and a close friend of the second marquis, was a member of a minor landed family with his own estate in county Down; he owned two houses and held the position of collector of customs in his own right. Reilly was from a middle-sized county Down landowning family and his father, a member of the Irish Parliament for the borough of Blessington, was also a close friend of the second marquis. The lesser Downshire agents, however – George Stephenson who managed the Castlereagh and Carrick-fergus estates for a period of 38 years until his retirement in 1818, and John Murray who was agent in Blessington from 1819 until his death in 1841 – were not the social equals of Matthews or Reilly.[17]

During the years of the third marquis's minority, the Blessington agent or 'receiver of rents' was Hill Benson, the vicar of St Mary's Church. He had a rather relaxed attitude to his position. In the earliest extant letter to his employer, written in September 1809 when the marquis had just come of age, the style was often fulsome and even gossipy. However, a more harassed note soon crept in, with the agent at pains to assure the marquis that he was working

55 Start of Hill Benson's letter to the marquis

very hard at his duties. In December the marquis bluntly expressed his dissatisfaction, pointing out that not one farthing of the November rents had been lodged to his bank account – and neither had he received accounts for the previous two years. He wanted to know what tenants were in arrears 'that I may prevent in future any person from literally cheating me and alleging excuses for the non-payment of my right'. Hill Benson tried to excuse himself by pleading that he was not a man of business but the marquis remained unmoved, saying that he ought not to have accepted the position in the first place if he found he

56   *Part of the marquis's letter to Hill Benson*

could not execute the duties of his office. 'I shall certainly hold you and every one of my agents and their trustees also to the engagements entered into during my minority,' he wrote, 'and I advise you therefore to do me that justice which you engage to do.'[18] An ominous postscript added the warning that 'my patience is nearly exhausted and you will find it best for you to obey my orders'. Shortly after this Hill Benson was unceremoniously sacked.

His successor was Thomas Murray, who had acted as a part-time surveyor from the late 1790s, later being promoted to permanent surveyor, a job he combined with the agency of Blessington until 1819, and that of Edenderry from 1819 onwards. His brother John, who worked with him as an assistant surveyor, then became the Blessington agent.[19]

Elizabeth Smith did not think much of John Murray's abilities, describing him as a person of 'no energy, no abilities and no new lights', although on a personal level she viewed him more kindly.[20] Nonetheless he was to serve as Downshire's agent for over twenty years. Much of his life revolved around his job and in his correspondence with the marquis he always portrayed himself as the faithful servant: 'I need not say that we participate in every circumstance that adds happiness to your lordship's family and feel for the reverse,' he enthuses when enquiring about the marchioness's health.[21] He participated in major family events and was one of three Blessington people invited to Hillsborough to celebrate the wedding of the marquis's eldest son, the Earl of Hillsborough, to Caroline, daughter of Viscount Combermere, in 1837.[22]

Murray's dealings with the Hillsborough administration were not always smooth, and a close watch was kept on him. Although the marquis had a very clear view, summed up in 1821, of what the agent's job was all about – 'let the order be, reduce the arrear, obtain the rent punctually by fair means if possible, punish the refractory and dishonest, encourage the good tenant and keep every account clear and distinct' – putting principle into practice was not always easy.[23] A cynical contemporary noted that 'the landlords were sometimes decent men, they will tell you, but the agents were devils one and all'.[24] Although by the nineteenth century the opportunity for the agent to abuse his power had on the whole ceased, there was still some scope for personal gain, even with all the checks and balances the marquis had put in place. Unscrupulous agents could exploit their position in a number of ways – by delaying the transference of part of the rent collected or accepting backhanders from people seeking preference on a holding or a more advantageous lease. Certainly Murray was under constant pressure, especially in regard to the twice-yearly collection of rents and the transference of monies as quickly as possible. No wonder he felt the need from time to time to protest his loyalty: 'My brother and I are fully aware of the ample payment given to us by the marquis,' he wrote on one occasion, and 'I believe that we are as grateful and attached to his Lordship's interest as any other persons can be.' When Thomas was accused of defaulting on the Edenderry rents, suspicion also fell on John; he was obliged to denounce the actions of his brother, saying that after twenty years in the service and confidence of his employer 'it is injurious to me for him to be a defaulter as it leads your Lordship to suppose that I am in the same situation'.[25]

When John Murray died in 1841, four months after his 'excellent wife', they were both mourned as kind, worthy people who, as Mrs Smith put it, 'will be missed, humble as was their sphere, more than all the rest of the families in the neighbourhood'.[26] But when Murray's final account with the marquis was being settled, it emerged that he had been engaged in fast dealing, including taking money for leases. 'I am never told everything,' exclaimed an upset Downshire. 'John Murray was I fear not honest and took money from the tenants.' It also emerged that some of the tenants had grievances against the agent. Robert Mulligan from Haylands complained that Murray had taken half an acre from his holding to make a pathway to the mill to facilitate other tenants but that he dare not complain when the agent was alive.[27] Murray's twenty years of service to the Blessington estate ended, then, with a cloud over his name and he was not honoured by a memorial in St Mary's as were his two immediate successors.

The next agent was Henry Gore, who was already in Downshire's employment as agent for a small estate in Kilkenny, a position he had obtained on the recommendation of Lord Courtown. When he was appointed he moved his family to the agent's house in Blessington and combined both agencies. By all accounts, he was a kindly and conscientious man, described by Mrs Smith as 'just and firm and kind, liberal, industrious, patient, steadily pursuing his plans for general improvement without frightening the ignorant by over-rapidity; and with great

IT IS THE PRIVILEGE OF
A FEW FRIENDS
WHO LAMENT THAT THEIR INTERCOVRSE WITH HIM
WAS BVT BRIEF,
TO PLACE HERE THIS TABLET
IN MEMORY OF
HENRY GORE,
A JVST MAN AND AN EARNEST CHRISTIAN.

"*Though the righteous be prevented with death
yet shall he be in rest*
Let us labour therefore to enter into that rest".
BORN APRIL 1796, DIED JANVARY 1843.

57　The Gore memorial in St Mary's Church

influence over Lord Downshire, an influence gained by the value of character'. When he died suddenly in 1843, his wife and her large family were expected to vacate the agent's house. The marquis, 'not being a man of any attachments except to his purse', according to Mrs Smith, declared that he would not wish on any account to disturb the family but 'confessed he did not like this interregnum'. He was anxious to have the new agent installed in the agent's house as soon as possible and expressed pleasure when he heard the news that the widow would shortly be leaving.[28] It would seem that although Downshire's agent was expected to be loyal to his employer, his family could expect little consideration on his death.

Gore was replaced as agent by William Owen. William Merrey, who was bailiff and under-agent to both Murray and Owen, gave a glowing report on the latter to the marquis. He considered Owen to be 'straightforward and businesslike' in his approach and despite the fact that he now had to work much harder, he preferred his new boss to Murray who had kept him 'in the dark'. He also thought Owen was 'very kind and communicative to the tenants'.[29] Owen remained as Blessington agent until 1890. His wife, who had moved from the comforts of her north of England home to settle in Blessington on her marriage towards the end of the 1840s, was, as Mrs Smith noted dryly, 'a woman of the lower order of gentility ... incapable of comprehending our dashing ways' and had difficulty adjusting to 'the untidy dirt and fun of most uncomfortable Ireland'. She passed her days 'managing to admiration' her home to the appreciation of a 'swarm of tea and cake visitors' and driving about the neighbourhood in a pony carriage, which was 'just a cut above Mrs John Hornidge and her tub'.[30]

In 1849, Owen, like Murray some years earlier, lost favour. The reasons catalogued by Elizabeth Smith were 'his loves, his marriage, his nonsense afterwards, his carelessness about their (the marquis and his wife) visit and the auditors' dissatisfaction at the dilatory proceeding about the accounts', all which threatened his position as agent. He survived Downshire's displeasure, however, and when he died after over forty years' service he was commemorated by a memorial in St Mary's. The last of the Downshire agents was Anthony Maude who in the first decade of the twentieth century was to oversee the handing over of the Blessington estate to the tenants.

58 The Owen memorial in St Mary's Church

❧ 7 The Tenants

*'We were to them only the receivers
of a much grudged rent.'*

ELIZABETH SMITH

Just as there was a hierarchy among the landlord class, there were also different categories of tenants. With 50-100 acres (part of which he may or may not have sublet) and a substantial house, the 'strong' farmer enjoyed a good standard of living, and his family could aspire to careers in the church or the legal and medical professions. Beneath the strong farmer were tenants of varying degrees of prosperity and at the bottom of the social pile were smallholders of one to five acres, many of whom were indistinguishable from the even more numerous class of cottiers and labourers. The labourers were either bound or unbound. A bound labourer usually had an agreement whereby a farmer gave him regular work in exchange for a plot of ground on which he built his cabin and grew his potatoes. No money exchanged hands and if the labourer wanted cash he had to sell any surplus crop or get extra work. The condition of the unbound labourer was more precarious as he was dependent entirely on whatever work he could find; moreover, as he had to pay rent for his potato patch he was particularly vulnerable if the harvest was bad or work was scarce.[1] In the Blessington area, the only work available, apart from the quarries at Kilbride and Ballyknockan, was on the larger farms but in the mainly grazing economy of the area this was limited.[2] Employment in the houses of the gentry, always a boost to the well-being of the local inhabitants, was restricted in the Blessington area owing to the relatively few large houses and the fact that many landowners were absentee.

The tenants on the Downshire estate were a mixture of Catholic and Protestant and small and large holders. As was the case in most estates throughout the country, the descendants of the planters lived on the better quality land in the lowlands, while the poorer upland areas, the so-called 'Bally' townlands, were mainly the preserve of the indigenous Irish. This Gaelic/Planter distinction corresponded to a large extent with the religious division of Catholic and Protestant. At the time there was a pronounced difference in the way many landlords viewed Catholic and Protestant tenants. Protestants were seen as synonymous with agricultural improvement, while Catholics were regarded as fickle, lazy and untrustworthy people, who would rather defraud their landlord than improve their situation. This view was shared by the central administration at Hillsborough and agent Murray in Blessington who constantly expressed his desire to fix 'good and loyal Protestants on the estate'. In this context, we find the third marquis enquiring in the 1820s whether any of the tenants' sons from Kilwarlin on his northern estates had offered to go to Blessington.[3] A decade earlier, a tenant named George Smith had acquired land in Crosscoolharbour, which he named Kilwarlin Farm, so presumably he had been one of the Downshire northern tenants. Smith, who was acquainted with William Reilly, the chief agent in Hillsborough, held a special position in the hierarchy of the Blessington tenants and was treasurer of the Blessington Estate Agricultural Society. He did not become a long-term tenant, however; he left with his family for Van Diemen's Land (Tasmania) in 1833 and his departure was described as a 'serious loss to the country and society'. Around the same time, Murray was at a loss to know why three other Protestant tenants were also thinking of leaving the country and was inclined to put it down to either fear or 'want of industrious habits'. He was not discouraged, however, from

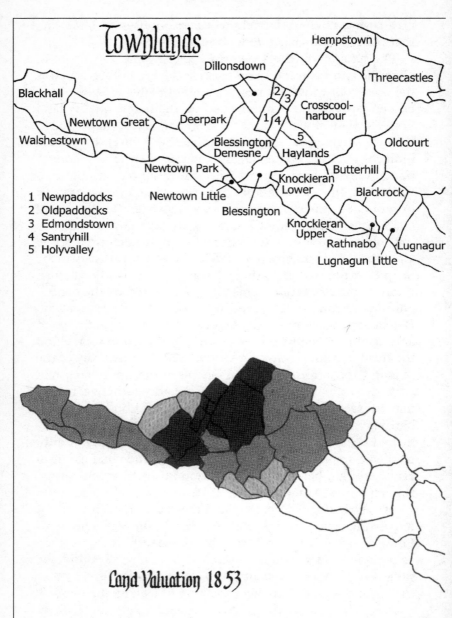

59 *Map of the townlands of the Blessington estate, with land valuations*

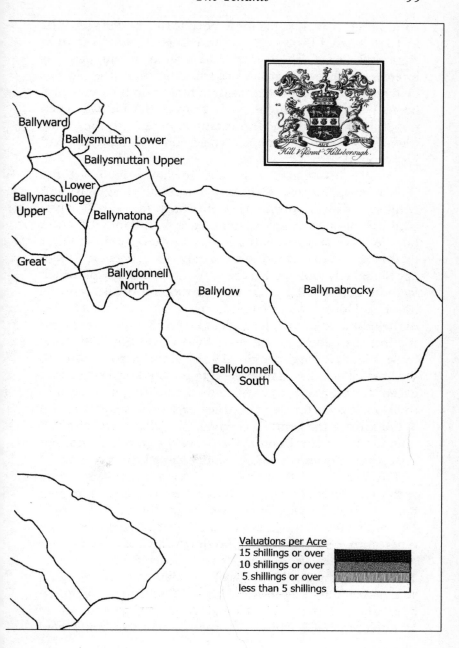

Ballyward

Ballysmuttan Lower

Ballysmuttan Upper

Lower

Ballynasculloge Upper

Ballynatona

Great

Ballydonnell North

Ballylow

Ballynabrocky

Ballydonnell South

Hill Viscount Hillsborough.

Valuations per Acre
15 shillings or over
10 shillings or over
5 shillings or over
less than 5 shillings

continuing to express his preference for Protestant tenants; in 1836 when a Protestant tenant wished to sell his farm in Butterhill to a Catholic who had offered to purchase his interest, the agent protested strenuously 'that it could not be disposed of except to a resident tenant on the estate and he to be a Protestant of good character'.[4] He was even hopeful of attracting Protestant tenants to the Bally townlands in the mountains, where some of the leases had just expired.

Families associated with the lowlands included the Boothmans, Eagers, Pantons, Fearises, Beaghans and Mullees. The Boothmans went back to 1707, when Thomas Boothman held a joint lease with Samuel Panton on the townland of Ballysmuttan Lower. By 1771, four members of the Boothman family had between them approximately 300 Irish acres, about 230 acres of which were in Crosscoolharbour. But by the end of the century, 'the Red House', one of their farms which contained 'some of the best land in the estate', had incurred large arrears and the interest had been sold to a John Cavanagh. When the lease went for tender in 1813, Boothman wrote to Downshire claiming a prior right to the holding, stating that except for the previous eight years the holding had 'been in their possession for two centuries past'. Cavanagh's action in bidding for the land, he claimed, was 'singularly base and ungrateful', as the Boothmans 'were the persons who first gave his family an acre of land and enabled them to stock'.[5]

The Fearis and Panton families were associated mainly with Threecastles and Crosscoolharbour and occupied fairly substantial farms in excess of 60 acres. Samuel Panton, who was the 'manor bailiff' at the beginning of the nineteenth century, had a holding in Crosscoolharbour 'which touches the Dublin road'. Joseph Eager held a 100-acre holding in Newtown Park, Benjamin Eager had a similar-sized holding in Rathnabo, William Eager acquired a substantial part of Blessington Demesne and all of Deerpark in 1812, while other members of the family lived in the town. The Beaghan family were associated with Blackhall and the Mullees with Newtown Great. Although the Boothmans, Eagers, Pantons, Finnemores and Beaghans retained ownership of their farms into modern times, other lowland tenants disappeared, and changing occupancy on the larger farms was a feature throughout the nineteenth century. In Crosscoolharbour, a holding of approximately 110 acres, which was originally leased by Rev Roger Miley, changed hands three times between 1810 and 1834. It was first acquired by William Walsh, then by George Smith, and when he emigrated it went to John and Michael Brown. Other tenants from Crosscoolharbour and Threecastles also disappeared from the estate. William Cavanagh, who held over 400 acres in three lots, was in difficulties from 1818, although no action was taken against him until ten years later when his land was put up for tender. The major part was acquired by Thomas Wilson, a brother of a landholder in nearby Elverstown in county Kildare and a 'cautious and industrious' person who, the agent believed, had the makings of a good tenant.[6]

In the marginal uplands, families were often concentrated in particular areas. The Hanlons were tenants in the neighbouring townlands of Knockieran, Blackrock and Butterhill, the Dowlings and Healys in Upper and Lower Ballynasculloge, and the Carney and Murphy families in Ballydonnell and Ballynatona respectively. James Murphy, who 'was born and reared' on a holding in Ballynatona was so attached to it that when he sought to retain it in 1809 he declared that 'he would rather give more for said land than any other'. He also wanted the adjoining holding for his father and asked George Ponsonby, who held the Kilbride estate at the time, to lobby the third marquis on his behalf. He was successful and Louis Murphy 'and partners' were given a 21-year lease on the townland; their descendants still retain land in the area. In Ballysmuttan Lower, the two Mullally families who held the townland were singled out by an estate evaluator in 1866 as being 'remarkable for

60 The third marquis on an inspection tour

their exertion in improving their holdings over the years.[7]

All the tenants were expected by the marquis to live up to certain standards. On a visit in 1829, he called them to a meeting and exhorted them to improve the appearance of their homesteads 'within and without' by the use of white wash and also to plant gardens and fruit trees. He was concerned that 'very few quick hedges' had been set and pointed out that shelter would be very advantageous for cattle and the growing of crops. He felt the estate could benefit from more labouring men and 'useful mechanics' but strongly discouraged 'travelling people' from settling there. No new dwellings were to be allowed upon the property 'but such as are occupied by the tenants or by their labourers'.[8]

Elizabeth Smith gives a graphic description of her first meeting with her tenants at Baltiboys House: 'There stood to welcome me a crowd of, as I thought, beggars – dirty queer-looking men doffing their remnants of hats with much civility. "Thim's the tenants," said the only man amongst them with a whole coat.'[9] Indeed there was hardly

61 Contemporary sketch of Irish peasants

a nineteenth-century visitor or commentator who was not appalled at the living conditions of Irish peasants. Most lived in one or two-roomed cabins of mud or stone without chimneys or glazed windows, and lean-to shacks erected at the side of the road were not uncommon. They were often clothed in an outlandish assortment of cast-offs which provided ready fodder for the English satirical journals of the day. When the harvest was good the majority had an ample if unvarying diet of potatoes, supplemented with milk or buttermilk but meat was a luxury enjoyed by few.

Extreme destitution was common in the marginalised areas in the west of the country. In 1837, a year before Lord George Hill, the brother of the third marquis, purchased an estate in Gweedore in county Donegal, the local schoolmaster, Patrick McKay, was so affected by the destitution he saw all around that he petitioned the Lord Lieutenant to alleviate the condition of the people in the parish. McKay, who was a well-travelled man familiar with many parts of Ireland as well as England, Scotland and North America, had never seen 'such hunger, hardships and nakedness' as he found in Gweedore. The inhabitants, he claimed, possessed between them 243 stools, 93 chairs, two feather beds, and their cabins had not more than ten square feet of glazed window between them. Their clothing was meagre, many were in filthy rags, and even in winter the children were often naked and half the population went barefooted. In addition, families rarely had more than one bed so that grown sons and daughters slept 'in the bare buff' with their parents, and the inhabitants shared their one-roomed cabins with the cattle.[10] He estimated the population of the parish as 4,000 but it was probably twice that; the census of 1841 put the figure at 9,000.

For the tenants on the Blessington estate, the quality of life varied. In the lowlands, conditions were relatively prosperous, the holdings were generally larger, subdivision was not so marked and the proximity of Dublin and the local quarries provided work. They also supplied the stone for building; thatched stone houses were prevalent and in Crosscoolharbour and Threecastles the strong farmers mostly lived in slated two-storied houses with a range of outhouses. But the uplands were a different matter. In Ballylow, one of the remotest parts of the estate, the tenants lived in low, thatched, stone cabins, which in the late 1830s were in 'very bad repair'.[11] Their livelihood was based on the rearing of small black cattle but the high altitude of the land meant the cattle had to be moved to the lowlands during winter and spring 'at very high prices indeed' – otherwise 'such animals would inevitably decline, perish, and die'. Any profit had to be 'expended for their [cattle's] support in winter' and so the tenants appealed to the marquis for a reduction in rent. They argued that they were more disadvantaged than their neighbours in Ballynabrocky and Ballynatona, because they endured 'inconveniences and disappointments' owing to the lack of roads and bridges. They even claimed that 'their dead ... [often]

62 Interior of peasant cabin

63 Kitchen of well-to-do tenant

remained uninterred for six days by reason of the floods with which they were surrounded'. Access to Ballylow improved in 1844 when a new road and a bridge across the Ballydonnell brook were built to meet the crossroads at Ballynatona.[12]

The tenants on estates where the landlord was resident always had a better chance of improving their living conditions. At Kilbride, George Moore built dwelling houses for some of his tenants in the upland areas of the estate in the 1830s. On the de Robeck estate near Ballymore Eustace, the landlord gave rent allowances to his tenants to improve their holdings, resulting in the building of some neatly finished two-storied, slated houses.[13] Mrs Smith also did her utmost to improve conditions. First, she and her husband had the thatch on all the cabins repaired, then they put in windows and built chimney stacks – 'not all at once either, but little by little as people deserved help'. She felt that the rebuilding of Baltiboys House had inspired the tenants to improve their own dwellings, an aspiration which was 'gratified by degrees as we could afford it'. Seventeen years after taking possession of the estate, she reported that four two-storey farmhouses had been built and many of the tenants were living in comfortable three-roomed slated cottages.[14] In contrast, in Lacken, which was owned by the absentee Joy family from Belfast, about fifty smallholders lived in miserable cabins clustered irregularly around the village. Their only means of support, apart from their smallholdings, was grazing rights on the mountain for the few sheep from which they produced home-spun clothing.[15]

8 Rent and Arrears

'I never knew a wise landlord to go to law with a poor tenant.'

JOHN FOSTER

Unlike their counterparts in England, few Irish landed families had commercial interests to underpin the income from their estates and practically the only way an Irish landlord could increase his income was to raise the rents. It is no wonder therefore that the whole question of rents – how they were fixed and collected – became such an important issue in Irish history. One nineteenth-century observer declared that 'there is no country in Europe in which landlords are possessed of such unlimited power over their tenants than in Ireland'. This sums up the traditional view of Irish landlords as a predatory class who ceaselessly demanded higher rents, and resorted to wholesale evictions and clearances if tenants got into arrears. But this is not the full picture and the evidence from estate papers reveals the complexity of the landlord-tenant relationship. As rents were not uniformly fixed and could vary greatly, not only throughout the country but even within the same estate, this led to anomalies. On some holdings they were reasonably pitched while on others exorbitant or rack rents were demanded. This was especially so in the first half of the nineteenth century.

The Downshires, as was the custom on large estates, employed a professional surveyor – and this at least ensured a degree of uniformity on the Blessington estate. Prior to the appointment of Thomas Murray as surveyor in 1809, a bidding system was used to fix rents; when leases expired the holding went to the person making the highest offer, even if the result was to dispossess the previous occupant. The response of some dispossessed tenants suggests this was a relatively new procedure. In 1794 a 68-acre holding in Butterhill changed hands when the lease expired because the previous tenant, John Clarke, 'never proposed a rent equal to what the present tenant pays'. Some years later the sons of Laurence Connor, the former tenant of a holding at Rathnabo, 'were the lowest proposers for it, and seemed surprised at any one interfering with their land, as they affected to call it'; in 1810 the family directly appealed to the third marquis to have the holding restored to them but despite the support of George Ponsonby, a neighbouring landowner, they were unsuccessful.[1] The reaction of the Boothmans to the taking over of one of their farms has already been noted. But there were dangers attached to letting land to the highest bidder. When rents were pitched too high the landlord lost out if tenants defaulted in bad times. The system also tended to act as a disincentive to improvement, especially in the years prior to the expiration of a lease; the outgoing tenant was inclined to exhaust the soil in order to make the holding less attractive to others.

Despite the existence of a surveyor, a modified version of bidding continued to be used in Blessington as late as the 1840s, with other factors besides the rent being taken into account. In 1828 when one of the largest farms on the estate became available for letting a number of people tendered. The holding, however, was not given to the highest bidder; factors such as the amount of land already held by the proposer and the likelihood of his residing on the farm were also considered. The bottom line was the proposer's ability to farm the land productively and pay the rent on time. Based on the surveyor's findings the agent would make recommendations but ultimately it was the administration in Hillsborough that had the last word.

During the last half of the eighteenth century, prices for agricultural products increased and reached their peak with

64 Proposal for tenancy

the great demand for cereals during the Napoleonic Wars, when France, first under the series of regimes that were established following the French Revolution and then under Napoleon Bonaparte, was at war with England. However, as the rents on long leases remained fixed, these price increases favoured the middleman rather than the landowner; middlemen could increase the rents they charged their undertenants but the landowner could not. So by the end of the eighteenth century, there was a growing tendency among landlords not to renew leases. Middlemen were still granted leases for the land they occupied themselves but the holdings they had sublet until then reverted to the landowner. On the Downshires estate in the north Mary Sandys had granted leases for political reasons but under the third marquis leases were generally not renewed, except to favoured tenants and then for a shorter period of 21 years and one life. On the Blessington estate a similar policy was operated. When John Finnemore died in 1833 all his leases expired. None were renewed except that on his 345-acre farm in Ballyward, which continued to be held by the family. But the Finnemores, as long-established tenants on the estate as well as creditors of the third marquis, successfully obtained a longer tenure than most tenants – 31 years and three lives – when renewing the lease on Ballyward. John Murray, the agent, had evidently underestimated the strength of Finnemore's position when he claimed a few years earlier that John Finnemore was 'blind to his own interest ... [and] cannot expect any compliment from your lordship' because he had refused to lower his interest rates on a loan to the marquis in line with other creditors.[2]

At the end of the eighteenth century, the gross rental income from the entire Downshire estate in Ireland was about £30,000. By 1815, this had increased to £55,000, of which about £6,000 came from the Blessington estate, £8,000 from Edenderry and the balance from the northern estate.[3] This increase was mainly due to the higher rents obtained on the renewal of leases during the third marquis's minority and this upward trend continued because of the buoyancy in the market which meant that tenants were prepared to pay more for land. In 1809 the rent on a 284-acre holding in Kilwarlin in the north, which had just come out of lease after 80 years, increased from £31 12s to £361. In 1810 the opportunity arose to raise the rents on the two core townlands of the Blessington estate, the Demesne and Deerpark. The previous tenant, William Patrickson, had held 730 acres of these lands at an annual rent of £327; the new occupant, William Walsh, was asked to pay £850, an increase of almost 160 per cent. But in many cases the high rents were more than the tenants were able to pay. Walsh

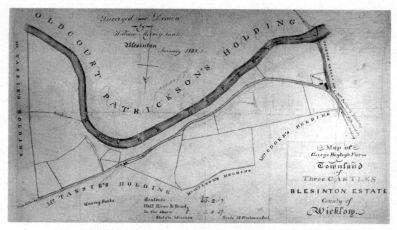

65 *George Begley's holding at Threecastles*

had to relinquish his tenancy a year later but the new
tenant, William Eager, also ran into difficulties. When
Walsh acquired Miley Hall around the same time, the rent
on this holding increased from £90 to £240 per annum and
within a few years he was forced once again to leave.

In 1815 the war with Napoleon ended and a sharp
agricultural slump followed, which was exacerbated by bad
harvests in 1816 and again in 1822. This brought famine to
many parts of the country and although Blessington did not
suffer as severely as other areas, the tenants' ability to pay
rents was affected and so arrears began to mount. In 1819
the half-yearly rent of £206 on William Cavanagh's
holdings in Crosscoolharbour and Threecastles remained
unpaid, as did the £3 7s 6d owed by George St Laurence
on his smallholding in Haylands. Soon the position became
so bad that the marquis accepted the inevitable and granted
a reduction of rent on many holdings on the estate. This
was not sufficient to ease the tenants' burden and a further
reduction was granted three years later. Some of the more
prominent tenants benefited from both reductions; William
Cavanagh's rents decreased by 17 per cent in 1819 and by
a further 19 per cent in 1822, while Thomas Fearis got an

overall reduction of nearly 30 per cent on the rent of £32
10s on his holding in Crosscoolharbour. The rent on Miley
Hall fell from £240 to £142 in 1822, and when a new
tenant took over some years later it was reduced further to
£115 per annum. The reduction on Blessington Demesne
and Deerpark was even more dramatic; William Eager now
paid only £346 per annum – almost the same amount as
was paid for the same land in the 1790s. In the uplands
lower decreases were the norm, amounting to only one-
tenth in some instances.[4] The net result of this was that the
overall rental income in 1824 was almost £1,000 less than
it had been in 1809 and remained at this level for a number
of years.

Throughout the 1820s and 1830s Hillsborough put
constant pressure on Murray to collect rents punctually and
recover arrears. Initially the agent tried gentle persuasion,
assuring the marquis that he lost 'no opportunity of
pointing out to the tenants how gladly they should pay all
they can to a landlord that has been so kind to them'. The
following year he stated that 'the tenants promise to pay
their rent by Christmas and also some of the arrears and I
will urge them as much as possible to do so'. But as
pressure from Hillsborough intensified he took a firmer
line. In 1825, he reported: 'I have served such of the tenants
as it was right to do so with notice to quit. They are
alarmed, which I hope will have a good effect on them as
well as those that were not served. I have also informed the
head tenants that unless the arrears on their farms is settled
that steps will be taken to recover possession.'[5]

Although such notices now became usual they were often
not acted on, serving merely to add the weight of the law to
the agent's efforts to collect arrears. Murray continued to
assure the marquis that everything possible was being done,
and between the second and seventh of December 1831
(the rents had become due in November) sent him a daily
report to tell him he was 'pressing them tightly'. By the end
of the month, acting on a directive from Thomas Parry, the

66 *Letter from John Murray about rents*

newly appointed accountant at Hillsborough, he made the
tenants in arrears sign an agreement to pay a sum equal to
half a year's rent along with their usual payment on each
gale day. He noted that 'this step has created alarm among
the tenants' and some had objected and wanted to pay only
a yearly sum of £2.[6] The tenants in the townlands of
Ballynatona and Lugnagun were particularly militant and
would not sign at all until Murray seized their cattle. But
little came of it all as the majority of tenants ignored the
agreement when paying their rents the following May. The
following year, three tenants in Blackhall were 'noticed' but
as estate documents show no action was taken in those
cases.

Various other strategies were attempted. Murray suggested that the tenants should take out life insurance to
cover arrears. This idea had been tried in January 1820,
when insurance on the life of John Walsh's mother was

transferred to the marquis as security for the arrears on his holding, and in 1832 was tried again when the arrears of Thomas Perry in Blessington were covered by 'insurance on his mother-in-law's life for £100'. But the majority of tenants could not have afforded such a scheme and the idea does not appear to have been taken up to any great extent by Hillsborough. More successful was the action taken against eight tenants in Ballynatona who were employed on a plantation at nearby Ballynabrocky; their wages were set against their arrears on instruction from Hillsborough.[7]

Although the collection of rents in Blessington remained a difficulty, by 1845 the income from the estate increased to £6,347, again mainly due to the higher rents obtained when leases expired. In 1833, Finnemore's rent on Ballyward doubled from £72 to £144; in Hempstown there was a huge rise from under £20 to £333,[8] and George Tassie faced an increase from 8s to 11s an acre on his 200-acre farm. In addition, a small increase was levied on all holdings in the estate, varying between one and four per cent.[9]

The difficulties Murray experienced collecting rents and reducing arrears were sometimes compounded by the marquis himself. In the mid 1830s, Peter Fearis, whose family had a long association with the estate, was an old man who lived with his wife on his 80-acre farm in Crosscoolharbour. Without an heir there was little prospect that he could clear the arrears of £472 that had accrued prior to the rent reductions of 1819 and 1822. In January 1836, Murray, believing that Fearis was unable to pay his arrears and had not the means to improve his farm, stated his intention of taking most of the holding, leaving Fearis with 'not more than 20 acres'. He wanted the bulk of it to be given to two 'improving tenants', Brown and Wilson, who were neighbouring large farmers. He also hoped that 'decisive proceedings against him [Fearis] will be much use as an example to other of the tenants'[10] and in addition would demonstrate to Hillsborough that he could act with firmness and determination in the collection of arrears on the estate. Twelve months elapsed, however, before any action was taken.

It was not the first time that Murray and Fearis had clashed. Some time previously, when the marquis visited Blessington, Fearis had taken the opportunity to speak to him directly without first consulting the agent. Murray was incensed and wrote to the marquis denouncing Fearis's 'impudence'. Fearis now believed that this was the reason why he had been singled out 'as a victim of unmerited persecution'. In March 1837, with the threat hanging over him of losing much of his 'little hereditary tenement', he made his case 'with much pain' to the marquis: 'Mr Murray is actually going to take half my little farm and this constant threat held over me of ruin and beggary weakens my frame and has almost affected my heretofore robust constitution and has left my wife, the companion of my woes, now on a bed of sickness perhaps to bereave me of all the comfort this world can afford.' He was careful to point out that he did not wish to seem critical of the agent: 'Mr Murray certainly does well in putting everything to the most for your Lordship ... and I am glad to see him so worthy of your Lordships great concern'. But he also took the opportunity to assert his own loyalty: 'I would die at his [Murray's] back in enforcing your Lordship's rights'. Fearis ended his letter with an entreaty to 'have pity and let me on my feet with some certainly of my little farm ...Ah, My Lord write to him [Murray] and say don't disturb poor Loyal Fearis'.[11]

The marquis did not immediately interfere and by 5 May Murray had made his move. The agent reported that as Fearis had refused to 'relinquish the land and accept a smaller acreage' he had seized and sold his cattle 'to the value of approximately £25'. He added that when Fearis's crops were harvested they also would be distrained. A week later, Fearis again wrote to the marquis seeking his intervention and giving his own account of what happened; not alone were his cattle taken and sold but also the two horses he was ploughing with. One of his neighbours,

Crosscoolarbou 17 March 1837

My Lord — With much pain I respectfully write to Your Lordship My little hereditary tenement under Your Lordship is so dear to Me — I pay full value for it full as much as I can make of it without even a sufficiency of the essential comforts that hard work & human nature requires & since Mr Reilly settled it at the Now rent I have paid up punctually — Yet Mr Murray is actually going to take half My little farm & this constant threat held over Me of Ruin & beggary weakens My frame & has almost effected My heretofore robust constitution & has left My Wife, the companion of My Woes, now on a bed of Sickness perhaps to bereave Me of all the comfort this World can afford, My Lord, have pity & set Me on My feet with some certainty of My little farm — Mr Murray certainly does well in putting every thing to the most for Your Lordship & he knows I would die at his back

67 Letter from Peter Fearis about his farm

however, had 'kindly purchased everything for me' and returned the animals the day after the sale. He was alarmed by rumours that a legal ejectment was to be served on him 'on your lordship's positive orders' and that his cattle were to be sold again in a week. He added that neither he nor the neighbouring tenants in Blessington believed that the landlord had any knowledge of the 'cruel manner in which he was being treated'.[12]

By now local feelings had been aroused. Fearis had the support of the leading gentry of the neighbourhood and the marquis received a declaration, signed by Richard and John Hornidge of Tulfarris and Russellstown, the Rev Ogle Moore of Kilbride, John Finnemore of Ballyward, Henry Smith of Baltiboys and the Rev Foster, the curate of St Mary's, stating that Fearis was 'a man of industrious habits, loyal, sober and well-conducted'. Later in the month 'the priest Archer' denounced the treatment meted out to Fearis from the altar at Crosschapel.

The marquis was now worried. Murray had told him that an ominous event had taken place at the sale of Fearis's cattle; several 'whitefeet', members of the secret agrarian society, the Whiteboys, had attended and 'threatened and intimidated anyone that attempted to buy'. This may explain why a neighbour had bought the stock and returned them to Fearis's land within twenty-four hours.[13] Murray already knew that agrarian secret societies had some support among the tenants; in 1822 the hay and outoffices of the parish priest, Michael Donnellan, had been maliciously burnt because it was alleged that he and his curate had 'taken an active part in suppressing the ribbon system'.[14] That the secret societies had not gone away in the meantime is shown by the fact that around the time of the Fearis incident a young widow named Murphy from Ballynatona was put in jail 'to be tried at next assizes for Whiteboyism'.[15] Faced with the threat of agrarian unrest in the neighbourhood, the marquis had no choice but to advise Murray to back off. Fearis was left in possession of all his land and his arrears were 'postponed'. They were never paid. The administration may have been mindful of the words of John Foster, last Speaker of the Irish Parliament, who owned estates in county Louth; writing in 1784, he said, 'I never knew a wise landlord go to law with a poor tenant ... confidence and fair words will answer better than distrust and resort to law.'[16]

A year later, fears again emerged that a secret agrarian organisation was still active in the uplands. Murray concluded from an 'assemblage by night of certain bodies of men within the district and from other indications that the ribbon system has been introduced and is likely, unless checked, to make progress in this part of the county'. He requested more police and especially a patrol at night, declaring that the 'Ballynatonas will be found guilty and transported, they will be tried at next assizes'.[17] No further evidence of Whiteboyism emerged and, like Fearis, the widow Murphy and the other tenants in Ballynatona remained in possession of their land.

The ending of the Napoleonic Wars and the collapse of cereal prices saw a shift to cattle rearing. Cereals could be grown on small or large holdings but cattle rearing required larger, more viable units. Thus landlords sought every chance to merge or 'square-off' farms, and the expiration of leases presented them with the opportunity to rid their estate of smallholdings and undertenants. This process of consolidation often led to tenant agitation, especially when there were evictions.

Elizabeth Smith relates how she and her husband adopted a deliberate policy of consolidation at Baltiboys, which they put in place in the 1830s. This was to undo the damage of 'the negligent days of my brother-in-law and his careless agent', which saw the proliferation of 'miserable little patches of farms of seven or eight acres'.[18] Many smallholdings were eliminated before the mid-1840s, and the Great Famine facilitated the removal of the remaining

68 Cabins in marginal areas

'bad' tenants, who had long been a source of irritation to the owners. Mrs Smith had no doubt about the rightness of this policy, and in a letter written to her daughter Annie, almost fifty years later, admitted that 'we determined to get rid of all the little tenants and to increase the larger farms'. This did not happen all at once but as opportunity arose, and the Smiths managed 'this delicate business without annoying any one – or even causing a murmur'. The evicted tenants were compensated for any improvements made to the holding, and given the means to set up in suitable employment.[19]

The third marquis had always been determined to consolidate holdings, and so undertenants and cottiers were removed from the estate as the opportunity arose. But in 1837 he gave explicit instructions that smallholdings were to be amalgamated with adjoining farms to make larger units. Declaring that he 'must have a just feeling towards my estate', he wanted to stop the 'long established and absurd practice' whereby the outgoing smallholder auctioned the remaining interest on his lease. Subdivision, he maintained, had fragmented larger units, facilitated population increase and left the smallholders little better off than the 'labouring poor'.[20] Murray echoed his master's dislike of subdivision. 'Surely,' he stated, 'a man that looks to the future prospects of his family' ought to plan for his children's future, rather than sinking all into penury by giving each a portion of his holding and, moreover, leaving nothing 'to pay the owner of the soil'.[21] It was probably due in large measure to Murray's vigilance that smallholdings were not a general feature on the Blessington estate but were usually confined to specific townlands.

Consolidation was a two-edged sword; it benefited the tenants who got an increase in the size of their holdings but for those who were dispossessed it could mean annihilation. Not all those ejected left peacefully. As early as 1810 Hill Benson had met with sturdy resistance when he attempted to evict the widow O'Toole and her son who were 'cottiers on the late Mr Miley's land' in Crosscoolharbour, one of the best farms on the estate containing about 110 acres. Under cover of darkness the widow removed all the corn and hay and 'deposited it on different houses on William Patrickson's farm in nearby Oldcourt'. When the agent found out, he assigned a constable to guard the produce but that night about forty of Patrickson's tenants 'bound the constable and carried the goods away'. As a result Hill Benson declared that two of the tenants, Simon Lawler and Stephen Deevy, 'should be represented to their landlord'.[22]

In 1828, Crosscoolharbour was again in the news when Kerrigan, an undertenant of Samuel Panton, was moved off his land. Kerrigan, however, was a tenant of some means and agreed 'to leave it to arbitration what he is to get on quitting'.[23] Other tenants were less favoured and left the estate without trace; in the same year Murray noted that the 'old cabins at the entrance of the town are down' while 'Panton is getting down the others at Crosscoolharbour'.[24] In Hempstown, when the lease expired in the 1830s, the marquis took the opportunity to reorganise the farms in the townland to facilitate giving a lease of 126 acres to a neighbouring gentleman, William Brownrigg of Ardenode, near Ballymore Eustace, possibly a relation of James Brownrigg, a previous agent on the Edenderry estate. This meant evicting four of the eight occupants, 'mostly bad', according to Murray. Brownrigg, not surprisingly, was unwilling to take the farm without the goodwill of the former tenants, which Murray asserted 'is not easy to have' and so the matter had to be negotiated. An offer to transfer the dispossessed tenants to Ballynasculloge, a mountain townland just then out of lease, was rejected, provoking Murray to describe the tenants as ill-minded and 'too long accustomed to an idle life'. By October 1834, however, he was able to inform the marquis that the previous occupants and their families, about forty people in all, had left Hempstown and Brownrigg had taken possession of the land. Three of the dispossessed tenants in Hempstown were Cullens but another two members of that family, Matt Cullen and his mother, were allowed to remain in their home and to retain two acres for a short period after Brownrigg had taken possession of the land. Later, Murray reported that he had paid mother and son £25 16s 4d 'for old walls and 2 acres' because after she died it might be difficult to get rid of the son and his large family.[25]

Landlords, ever anxious about maintaining peace and good order among the tenants, were particularly concerned about political agitation, and throughout the first half of the nineteenth century the national political scene was dominated by one man – the Liberator, Daniel O'Connell. O'Connell had won this title by organising a mass political movement throughout the country which culminated in 1829 with the granting of Catholic Emancipation. Catholics were now given the right to hold senior official and legal positions and to sit in Parliament. O'Connell later turned his energies towards repealing the Act of Union and in 1843 he revived the technique of mass agitation, which he had

69 An O'Connell mass meeting

used so successfully in obtaining emancipation. This consisted of a network of local committees, a fund-raising scheme nationwide, close co-operation with the Catholic clergy and the use of newspapers to highlight his cause. It was a movement that worried many landlords and their agents.

In 1843, as the movement for repeal gained momentum, the Downshire agent, William Owen, kept a close watch on the situation in Blessington. He reported to the marquis that 'the enlightened' in Blessington did not expect trouble but 'the uneducated', on the other hand, believed that 'before the new potatoes are dry' the country would erupt. However, a mass meeting held in nearby Ballymore Eustace in June passed off without any noticeable effect on Blessington. Two months later, when a similar gathering was to take place at Baltinglass, Owen noted that the handbills posted up in Blessington to announce the event were removed quickly but he was nonetheless apprehensive because 'a great number of the agitators' were expected to breakfast in the town on their way from Dublin to

Baltinglass.[26] In the event the peace in Blessington remained unbroken but much curiosity was aroused. Elizabeth Smith encountered 'at least 150 people' who had walked to the main road to see O'Connell's carriage pass by, while Blessington itself 'was filled with a mob of the unwashed' who 'showing little enthusiasm' came from 'mere curiosity'. O'Connell, however, gave the assembled people little joy; he did not change horses in Blessington, as was the usual practice with carriages coming from Dublin, but 'drew down the blinds' and drove quickly through the town, without anyone 'raising a hat to him'.[27]

The arrest of O'Connell on charges of conspiracy the following November aroused fears of retaliation but once again Owen reported that with few exceptions 'people here are very quietly disposed' and little interest had been shown in the outcome of the trial.[28] However, three of 'your Lordship's Roman Catholic tenants', were willing to act as collectors for a church-gate collection for the benefit of O'Connell, which, with the support of the local Catholic clergy, was held after Sunday Mass in mid-November. Owen gave the tenants 'friendly advice' not to 'involve themselves in a conspiracy', and so without the marquis's name 'being mentioned in the matter', the tenants reconsidered their decision and 'their reverences' had to find collectors from outside the estate. The tenants, fearful of falling out of favour with their landlord and his agent, had capitulated. The following May O'Connell was imprisoned and on his release four months later went to the continent where he died in 1847.

9 The Landlord's Role

'Property has its duties as well as its rights.'

THOMAS DRUMMOND

A great landowner had enormous influence in his particular area. It touched on every aspect of life – developing the estate town, building roads, encouraging industry, promoting good agricultural practice and providing education. In Blessington, the layout of the town as we know it today, the road frontage of most of the houses and the dimensions of the accompanying sites have their origins in the plans drawn up by the first Marquis of Downshire in the 1780s which continued to be implemented by the second marquis. The entrance to Blessington House, opposite St Mary's, was recessed, thus creating the present town square, the main street was lengthened and widened at the Baltinglass end, and a new access to the Kilbride Road was created to replace Church Lane, the laneway previously situated between the church and what is now the hotel. The marquis encouraged the development of the town by granting leases for building and by the creation of town parks of three acres in which the residents could grow their own produce. The ground rent was 1s 0d a foot, estimated on the road frontage, while the rent on the town park was one guinea an acre. The marquis also built a post-office and provided sites for a new inn and a market house. A few favoured people shared in the building development: Charles Lilly, who had worked on the refurnishment of Blessington House, erected three two-storied and three one-storied houses; agent William Patrickson built a number of houses and a barracks, and his brother John acquired sites including 'one of the most eligible situations for building on' (now occupied by AIB).[1] But all this development stopped with the 1798 rebellion and the town lay in ruins for several years.

Blessington began to recover around 1809 when the third marquis took control. The burnt-out houses were rebuilt and several people including George St Laurence, Charles Doran, James Kelly and Benjamin Eager tendered for sites. St Laurence, who was in partnership with Doran, initially wanted a house next to Walsh, the publican, 'as a spot to reside in' while he was engaged in constructing houses. Other sites which were developed included one 'above Mr Trousdall's house', a second which had been the old market house next to St Mary's Church, and a third which is now occupied by West Wicklow House.[2]

Despite the damage caused by the rebellion, Blessington still had the many services required in a small town – a mill, post-office, victualler's shop, public house, bakery, inn and grocery shop. Alexander Burke was in charge of the post-

70 View of Blessington in 1857

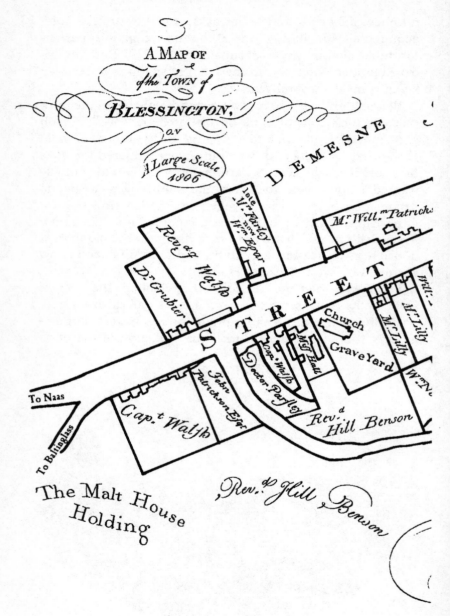

71 Longfield's map of Blessington in 1806

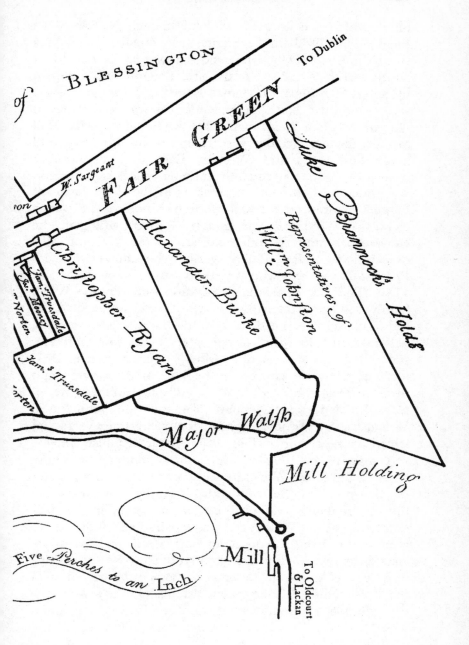

office which was located on land known as 'Sergeant's Field', while William Sergeant, the victualler, lived in a slated house for which he paid a low rent of 6d a foot because of the small size of the site. The mill was occupied by an elderly gunsmith, James Rainsford, a member of a well-established estate family, whose son was an attorney in Dublin. Stephen Walsh owned the public house, Miss Hall ran the bakery 'to the great comfort of the town and neighbourhood', and William Eager, 'a very sober industrious and consequently thriving man', kept the inn and grocer's shop.[3] Other notables in the town included Samuel Panton, the bailiff, Joseph Mooney, the parish clerk, Mr Trousdall, the guager, Robert Mulligan, the gamekeeper, and several members of the Walsh family, descendants of Rev Philip Walsh 'who came over with Primate Boyle' and who was the vicar between 1698 and 1736. This began a long association between the Walsh family and the estate. Philip's wife Catherine lived to the age of ninety-five and died from 'decay' in 1769, outliving her husband by thirty-three years. His son, William, succeeded him as vicar of St Mary's and was married first to Mary Stewart, 'couzon to the Earl of Blessington and niece to Dean Stewart', and secondly to Elizabeth Ravell from Woodend near Oldcourt. William's son, John Ravell Walsh, was curate in the parish for twenty-four years and later became rector of Tubber and vicar of Gillstown. He was married in 1792 to Euphemia Prendergast, whose father acted as an official in the Court of Chancery under the first marquis. He lived with his family in a substantial house, originally built by the marquis as an inn. It was damaged in the rebellion but was repaired and fitted out to receive the Lord Lieutenant, Earl Hardwick, when he visited the town. John died from typhus in 1833 at the age of 81 and is buried in Blessington. Two other members of the Walsh family, all clergymen, also lived in the town in the early decades of the nineteenth century. William converted what had previously been a gardener's house on the demesne land into a 'commodious cottage in which he dwells and has made several useful buildings about it', while his brother 'wishing much to have a holding in the estate' was given part of the land to the 'west of the great avenue to the park' but 'does not occupy himself but sets to different people'.[4]

By the late 1830s, markets were regularly held in the town and so the third marquis decided to build a market house, which would include a magistrate's assembly room and a jury room on the first floor. In 1838, a contract was drawn up detailing all aspects of the construction and the builder, Patrick Kearney, had to sign a guarantee disowning any association with ribbonmen or other unlawful organisations. Kearney, described 'as a loyal subject', was to complete the project 'in a manner creditable to me as a tradesman and advantageous to the Lordship of Blesinton'. The construction and material costs for the building, which did not include Kearney's profit, was estimated at nearly £800. Experienced stonecutters were paid £1 per week, other stonecutters received from 15s to 18s according to their abilities, men working in the quarries got 10s, while common labourers were paid 1s per day. The ready availability of local materials was an essential element in keeping down costs, and there was a source of cut stone close at hand in Boyle's ruined mansion, situated 'about a quarter mile and not much hill' away. Since 'the internal part or face of exterior walls' of the big house were 'all nearly down or fractured' and the outside was 'liable to fall when disturbed', great care was required in removing the stones.

By August 1838 Kearney had started on the project but things did not run smoothly. Although the Downshire accountant, Thomas Parry, had described the progress on the building as 'a real pattern of work', the marquis was less enthusiastic. First, he wanted the foundation raised, then as the work was not proceeding quickly enough he rebuked Kearney for his 'want of punctuality' and for breaking his

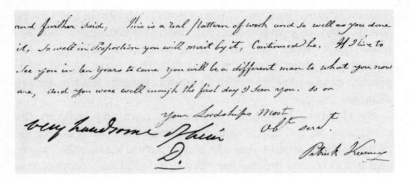

72 Kearney's letter, with the marquis's comment

contract. He felt the builder was acting from bad advice, and it would do him no good 'to injure or annoy me who have never done him any harm at all but the reverse'. Kearney, he concluded, was no better that any of his countrymen – 'the crooked ways so common in Ireland are the ruin of its people'.[5] It is not clear when the market house was finished but a part of the original weighing-scales, which still survives, dates from 1845.

In the nineteenth century, the only church in Blessington was St Mary's, built by Archbishop Boyle.[6] The Catholic church was at Crosschapel and had been built in the 1770s in the townland of Crosscoolharbour, three kilometres outside the town. It stood on the site of the present church on land previously held by the Neville family of Furness, near Kilteel in county Kildare, which was given to the 'Romanish' before the estate came into the possession of the Downshires. The first marquis was a benefactor of the church and gave '20 guineas towards the building of it'.[7] Roger Miley was parish priest there from 1773 until his death in 1801 and is commemorated by a plaque in the church. He was a man of substance who was granted a lease on a 110-acre farm in Crosscoolharbour in 1775, and expended upwards of £1,200 on building a house, Miley Hall, and in addition extensively planted the land with trees.[8] He also held land in the Demesne as well as 250 acres at Tinode in the parish of Kilbride, which he sublet to undertenants. On his death his nephew, Miles Miley, inherited the farm in Crosscoolharbour and also succeeded him as parish priest in Crosschapel – at the time it was not unknown for particular parishes to be the preserve of the same family and the position of parish priest could pass from uncle to nephew. Miles Miley allowed the farm to 'go much into disorder' and reset some of it to undertenants. When he died in 1809 – according to tradition following a fall from his horse close to his house in Red Lane – his brother John took over the tenancy. 'By cutting, selling or giving away trees off it', John in turn allowed the property to devalue further and he was eventually faced with ejection when the lease expired. He finally 'gave possession' in 1810 but refused to leave immediately, and the new tenant, Walsh, did not take over until a year later.

Miles Miley was succeeded as parish priest by Michael Donnellan, who sought a site in Knockieran, nearer to the town, on which to build a church and a permanent house for the priest of the parish. He was unsuccessful but was

73 Church of Our Lady at Crosschapel

given instead 19 acres adjoining the church at Crosschapel, which was taken from Patrick Farrell's farm. The marquis also assured Donnellan that he would 'be very happy in contributing to the comfort and happiness' of his tenants including 'those of your persuasion' and hoped that a contribution of fifty guineas towards the building of a 'glebe house for the Catholic clergyman' would be acceptable.[9] In 1834 another parish priest, Francis Archer, again looked for a site in the town for a new church but the agent was against it, arguing that the existing church could be enlarged and that together with the chapel in Kilbride it was sufficient for the needs of the Catholic tenants.[10]

In nineteenth-century Ireland, good roads were essential to the prosperity of an area, as it made travel and com-munication easier, and opened up new markets. To build or improve a road the co-operation of local landowners was necessary, so the third marquis, a keen supporter of progress, instructed his agent to negotiate on his behalf in promoting road-building projects. He was particularly interested in the road through Blessington, which he wanted to have designated as a mail-coach road linking Dublin and Waterford, via New Ross. With this in view, he personally lobbied people of influence, including the Post Master General, Sir Edward Lees, arguing that the route would be shorter than the existing one which went through Naas.[11] In 1813 work started on upgrading 'the new line of road'. One of the biggest challenges was the construction of a bridge over the gorge at Poulaphouca, which was undertaken by Alexander Nimmo, a well-known engineer of his day, who also built many harbours in the west of the country as part of famine relief schemes. By 1823 a sum of £25,000 had been expended and Murray was able to report to the County Wicklow Grand Jury that the bridge was 'now in a state of great forwardness and the road through county Wicklow nearly completed'. Work on a three-mile stretch through the 'Commons of Saggart' in county

74 *The Nimmo bridge at Poulaphouca*

Dublin, however, was being 'impeded by local interest'.[12]

The marquis did all he could to speed up the work and had Murray present a memorandum to the Lord Lieutenant, which he and Murray signed, together with Lord Aldborough of Baltinglass, the Hornidges and Finnemores, Baron de Robeck's agent, Matthew Lynch, and two Catholic curates, Michael Toole and Charles Sinnott. The agent also canvassed the support of Mr Cobbe, the owner of an estate in Glenasmole in county Dublin who had influence with the County Dublin Grand Jury, pointing out that the new road 'will be of benefit to his tenants' and therefore should have his support.[13]

By 1828, Murray could report to the marquis that a 'caravan', which had space for 16 passengers and was generally full, 'leaves Dublin for Tullow every morning, arriving in Blessington at 10 o'clock'. Similarly a coach from Tullow 'passes through Blessington at 1 pm. every day'. Murray also reported on the amount of traffic passing through the town during a seven-day period in July of the same year. In the space of one week, 96 carriages and 869 carts as well as a variety of farm animals were recorded.[14] The following year, the progress of the 'new line of road' was still engaging the agent's attention and he canvassed Major Humphrey, Lord Wicklow's agent, for support, while Lord Aldborough promised to lend £1,000 to further the project. The road took a long time to complete, for as late as 1834 the agent was communicating with landowners as far away as Borris in county Carlow.[15]

The marquis was also interested in improving the road linking Blessington to Roundwood, which had been in existence since before the 1790s, and so he contributed £50 towards the part that went 'through the Lordship of Blessinton'. This road, which passed through Oldcourt and the Liffey valley to cross the mountains at the Sallygap, still serves today as one of the two links between east and west Wicklow and lives up to Murray's description of it as being 'a delightful one and a great utility'.[16]

When the Liffey bridge at Ballyward, at the boundary of the Downshire and Kilbride estates, was in need of repair, the marquis hesitated before contributing anything. John Finnemore had already subscribed £30 towards its reconstruction but the marquis wanted to know what Ponsonby, the Kilbride landlord, would pay before committing himself. He agreed to 'give whatever Mr Ponsonby gives, both estates being accommodated'. In the end each gave 50 guineas, and in October 1815, the bridge was declared open but a year later more money was sought from the Wicklow Grand Jury to complete the battlements.[17]

Progressive landlords in eighteenth and nineteenth century Ireland were also interested in promoting industries, in many cases providing the capital. In the late eighteenth century the Earl of Aldborough had developed a textile industry around his newly planned village at Stratford-on-Slaney south of Blessington. In 1810 a proposal by James Jackson, a farmer, and Henry Campbell, a cotton manufacturer from Stratford-on-Slaney, to set up a similar

industry in Blessington, was turned down. Murray, who
had the responsibility of assessing the viability of such
projects, concluded that the venture was not in the interest
of the estate at the time. His decision may have been
influenced by the failure of a small textile enterprise, which
a Mr Mahony had established in Blessington some time
earlier. Mahony disappeared leaving arrears of rent but
Murray felt that the estate was well rid of that 'eccentric
person'.[18] In 1829 a more ambitious proposal was made by
a Mr Caffrey who expressed an interest in investing
upwards of £10,000 in 'a worsted spinning and cloth
factory'. Caffrey had a similar business elsewhere but the
fuel for its steam-driven machinery was costing him £500
annually. He believed that the running costs on a river site
in Blessington would be considerably less and the rates of
pay for labour cheaper. He tried to drive a hard bargain with
the agent, demanding 100 acres of land adjoining the
existing mill, then in a state of decay, and a lease for 99

75 The old mill

years at a low rent. Murray kept in close contact with the marquis about the matter but once again caution prevailed. 'It must be always kept in view,' Murray declared, 'to keep off an increase of population that might hereafter impoverish the estate'. The development of the mill site was left hopefully for more prosperous times, with the marquis optimistically noting that the fall on the bend of the Liffey at Blessington 'will some day, if well managed, both pay well and be of service to the estate'– a hope which never materialised.[19]

Over the years, a number of small enterprises had been located at the mill site. The gunsmith James Rainsford held the property in the first decade of the nineteenth century' but by 1822 it had changed hands. The new owner, William Merrey, was a well-established employee of the estate, holding the position of bailiff and later that of under-agent. He now established a needle manufacturing business on the mill site, but his enterprise did not thrive. When the Hillsborough administration wished to purchase needles from him he had difficulty meeting the order as 'those he employs do not know the business sufficiently'. All Murray could promise was that the order 'will be filled when he [Merrey] can finish them in the best manner'. It comes as no surprise that shortly afterwards the agent was seeking a new tenant for the mill. Merrey, however, was still in possession in the early 1830s and it was not until some years later that a Mr Ebbs took over the site and ran it as a corn mill for the neighbouring farmers.[20]

The nineteenth century saw many changes in agricultural practice in Ireland. When the Dublin (later the Royal Dublin) Society was founded in 1731 it encouraged the establishment of local agricultural societies and helped to create a growing awareness of the need for improvement. New agricultural techniques such as the Scottish iron plough, which was far superior to the old Irish wooden plough, the use of drills instead of ridges for cultivation, and scythes instead of sickles and hooks now made their appearance. Threshing and reaping machines also became available, and a better understanding of the importance of drainage, crop rotation and the need for fertilising became more common in farming circles. The new methods were taken up by the more viable, commercial farmers, especially cereal growers, and the pioneers were often younger, better educated and of a higher social class than the average farmer. In 1830, at the agricultural show in Skibbereen in county Cork, only five iron ploughs were to be seen, but by 1846 that number had increased to 28.

The new techniques did not immediately replace the older traditions, particularly on poor land in the upland areas. The expanding population, combined with the growing determination of landlords to create fewer and larger holdings, put enormous pressure on land, and so dispossessed tenants were often given tracts of hitherto uncultivated bog and mountain where the older methods of cultivation were more suitable. The traditional Irish wooden plough was better than the new Scottish one on wet and undrained land, ridge cultivation could be varied to suit the slope of mountain land, while rain-flattened crops – a not uncommon phenomenon in Ireland – could best be harvested using the old-fashioned sickle and hook.[21]

The existence of a farming society in Blessington in the 1820s and the holding of ploughing competitions suggest that the Downshires were aware of the benefits of the new farming techniques. The family had always been interested in agriculture and the first marquis was noted as an improving landlord. The third, and later the fourth, marquis inherited this interest and both were actively involved in the Royal Dublin Society. When the first farming society established in Blessington fell into decline, Murray, probably at the marquis's instigation, proposed the setting up of a new one. His first task was to establish a committee and to this end he approached John Finnemore, who at first refused to join. Nonetheless, he assured the

THE
BLESINTON ESTATE
FARMING SOCIETY;

Patron,
THE MOST HONORABLE THE MARQUIS OF DOWNSHIRE;

Presidents,
JOHN FINNEMOR AND JOHN MURRAY;

Treasurer,
GEORGE SMITH;

Secretary,
ROBERT PANTON.

PREMIUMS,
PROPOSED FOR THE YEAR 1830:

1.—To the Farmer—his Son, or his Brother, residing with him—holding their own Plough, who shall plough half a Rood of Ground in the best manner, with his own pair of Cattle, and without a Driver, not more than eight inches wide, and not less than five inches deep, in three hours,

First Premium,	....	*An Iron Plough;*
Second ditto,	....	*A Harrow;*
Third ditto,	....	*Harness for a Pair of Cattle.*

2.—To the Farmer's Servant who shall plough half a Rood of Ground in the best manner, and with the greatest ease to the Cattle, with Neat Cattle, Horses, or Mules, and without a Driver, not more than eight inches wide, and not less than five inches deep, in three hours,
First Premium, £1—Second do. 15s.—Third do. 10s.—Fourth do. 5s.
The Ploughman must be at least Three Months in the service of the Person who sends the Plough.

3.—To the Farmer who shall have his Ground and ditches cleanest from Weeds,

First Premium,	....	*A Wheel-barrow;*
Second ditto,	....	*Garden Sheers and Bill-hook;*
Third ditto,	....	*Spade and Shovel.*

4.—To the Farmer who shall make the greatest number of Perches of Ditching, not less than 100 in the year 1830, well quicked with Thorn and Forest Trees (Oak), planted in the breast ten feet asunder,
First Premium, £1—Second do. 10s.—Third do. 5s.
The Fences must be straight, and made in a workmanlike manner.

5.—To the Labourer, or Tradesman, not holding more than Four Acres of Ground, having their Cottage and Garden in the neatest and best order,
First Premium, £1—Second do. 10s.—Third do. 5s.
The Cabins must be Whitewashed twice in the year, and no Manure left in front of them.

PREMIUMS FOR SPINNING AND KNITTING.

6.—To the Woman, assisted by her Children, residing with her, who shall spin the greatest quantity of Flax, not less than 40 lbs. in the year 1830,
First Premium, £1—Second do. 15s.—Third do. 10s.—Fourth do. 5s.

7.—To the Woman, assisted by her Children, residing with her, who shall knit the greatest number of Pairs of Stockings, full sized, and not less than 40 Pairs,
First Premium, £1—Second do. 15s.—Third do. 10s.—Fourth do. 5s.

A Farmers' Dinner will be provided, at the Downshire Arms Inn, Blesinton, on the Day of the Ploughing Match, at 4s. per Ticket for each Person.

76 Blessington Farming Society poster of 1830

agent that he would subscribe to the society but wanted first to see what other tenants would pay before committing himself to a specific amount.[22]

The inaugural meeting was held in November 1829 and Murray read an address from the marquis before the election of a committee made up of 'the tenants from the different parts of the Lordship'. Two of the larger tenants, George Smith and Robert Panton, were appointed treasurer and secretary respectively, while Finnemore, who had now changed his mind about joining, became co-president along with Murray. The following year the new Blessington Estate Farming Society held its first show. There was a ploughing competition and premiums were granted to the farmers for keeping weeds under control and for digging ditches and planting hedges on their holdings. There were also prizes for the neatest and best-kept house and garden, as well as for knitting and spinning.[23]

Murray, who was convinced that the improvement of the land 'should never be lost sight of', encouraged the tenants to sow rape, turnips, vetches and a mixture of different grasses. The planting of potatoes in drills and the use of lime are mentioned in his letters and show that such practices were becoming more widespread. The improvement of the breeding stock on the estate was also his concern and when the third marquis enquired about the condition of some animals on a particular farm, Murray was able to assure him that the tenant in question, Eager, looked after the hoggets, fed them on turnips and bran and housed them at night. The marquis also gave incentives to the tenants to improve the quality of poultry – 15s, 25s and 30s for the production of turkeys of 20, 25 and 30 lbs in weight. Murray astutely noted that since it was difficult to rear fowl up to 20 lbs the premiums were unlikely to be claimed. The real purpose of the exercise, he concluded, was 'to encourage people to try what might be done', although he could not resist the thought that it could be a case of getting credit 'without losing anything'.[24]

Murray's policy of supporting agricultural improvements was continued by his successors, notably William Owen who had 'large farming concerns' in county Kilkenny. Shortly after his appointment to Blessington in 1843, Owen attended a meeting of the Royal Agricultural Society in Dublin, where a letter from the marquis 'got a good deal of consideration'. The same year the marquis invited Owen to attend the agricultural show at Hillsborough and encouraged him to visit farms near Warwickshire where he saw 'farming carried on in fine style and on a bold scale' which was 'well worth the seeing by an Irishman'. Previously he had advised the marquis on how to farm the Demesne and Deerpark. 'The rich land next the town' would if 'treated to a surface dressing' be ideal for the feeding of cattle and the occasional 'finishing of sheep'. Store or breeding sheep with some 'growing' cattle, fed with turnips in the winter, were best suited to the Deerpark, while the land in between was ideal for growing green crops 'for the support and finishing of different kinds of stock and the production of manure'.[25]

Land reclamation was another topic of the day. In 1837, Rev William Hickey made a proposal on behalf of his son to reclaim part of Ballynabrocky townland on the eastern fringe of the estate. He was a close friend of the Moores who some years before had taken over the Kilbride estate and undertaken an extensive drainage scheme across the Liffey from Ballynabrocky. Hickey envisaged a similar scheme, which would have involved the removal of five tenants then occupying the townland and the payment of upwards of £700 to gain 'their goodwill'. In the event the enterprise did not go ahead. Murray, on the advice of William Brownrigg, the new tenant of Hempstown, argued that Hickey was a bad risk, while Hickey retaliated that 'his son would not venture to establish himself in so wild a neighbourhood'.[26]

The upper reaches of Ballynabrocky were already the focus of one of the largest projects undertaken on the estate, the planting of 500 Irish acres with trees. A monument, still to be seen in this barren and wild landscape, states that the plantation was to be known as Coronation Plantation to commemorate the accession of King William 1V in 1830. It was an enterprise in which the third marquis took a keen interest and was frequently reported on by Murray. The work commenced in 1831, with tenants from nearby Ballynatona employed on the scheme. By October 1834 7,000 oaks as well as poplar cuttings had been planted and later that year Murray acknowledged the receipt of two casks of acorns, which led to the planting of a further 20,000. In April 1837 the planting of oak and Scots fir was held up due to inclement weather.[27] It is not known exactly when the planting at Ballynabrocky ceased but the eventual scale of the operation was more modest than first envisaged. The plantation was of little economic benefit to the Downshires but during the First and Second World Wars it was a valuable source of fuel for the local community. Today all that remains of the project are the original monument and a few pine and oak trees.

It was widely held in the nineteenth century that one of the main obstacles to progress was lack of education. Ignorance was considered an impediment to schemes for improving the life of the tenants and to their developing habits of industry and initiative. Consequently, progressive landlords saw the advantages of building and endowing schools. Penelope, wife of Charles Dunbar, great-great-grandson and inheritor of Archbishop Boyle's estate, had established and endowed a school in Blessington in the last quarter of the eighteenth century. The Hills continued the Boyle tradition and the third marquis not only took responsibility for the upkeep of a school and the salaries of the teachers but also showed an interest in the pupils and in what they were taught.

The Blessington school opened at 9 am and finished at 4 pm every day. Religious instruction was emphasised, with the bible, psalms and catechism being studied. The original charter of the school, 'not to admit any but Protestant children residing on the Lordship of Blessinton', was not stringently enforced but Catholic pupils were expected to attend Church of Ireland services in St Mary's. In 1819, when about twenty Catholic boys were dismissed for non-attendance at church and school, the agent sought a ruling from the marquis. Subsequent reports show that no ban was placed on Catholics, so the church attendance clause was probably quietly dropped.

The same year, the marquis spent more than £60 on the school, including the master's salary of £15, and money for hats, shoes and stockings for the pupils. A report from Murray gave details of the pupils' progress. Henry Norton, who had been a pupil for almost four years, had reached the 'rule of three in fractions', John Redmond, a student for a similar length of time, was engaged 'in multiplication of divers denominations', and James Gyves, a first-year pupil, was working at 'reading, spelling, writing and figures'. The teacher was the elderly Dr Parsley, 'a useful member of the medical proffession', who was 'for many years an instructor of youth in the town'. He was esteemed by the third marquis, who personally commissioned a plaque in his memory in St Mary's. In 1828, a sizeable proportion of Catholics, both boys and girls, were attending and a school inspector rated it 'a most useful establishment'.[28]

In 1831, the National Board of Education was set up and a country-wide network of national schools came into operation. The landowners were among the Board's strongest supporters; Lord Erne made regular payments to the schools at Lifford, Sir George Hodson helped to build three schools on his Cavan estate while Lord Inchiquin paid the salary of one of the local teachers.[29] The Board gave a grant of £60 for the establishment of a separate girls' school in Blessington. However, for large numbers of Catholic children the only form of education available at the time was in the hedge-schools, which owed their name to the habit of holding classes out of doors in the summer; in the winter time they were held in a barn or outhouse provided by a local farmer.[30]

For a time the two systems of education – national schools and hedge-schools – existed side by side, sometimes amicably, sometimes not. Mrs Smith, who had established a new national school on her estate, complained that the main obstacle to its success was the local curate, Father Rickard, who was setting the people against it. In the early 1840s she complained to Dr Murray, the Catholic Archbishop of Dublin, and as a result Rickard was removed but the parish priest, Father Germaine, continued to be uncooperative. Rumours had been circulated in the parish that Mrs Smith had burnt the Catholic catechism, with the result that many of the pupils had left her school. The teacher, Miss Gardiner, was so distressed about the allegation that she wished to confront Father Germaine who was reported to be 'determined to make a great noise about it'. Mrs Smith told her to take the matter coolly and if the parish priest called on her to say that the rumours were ill-founded as 'there were no catechisms in the

77 A hedge school

school, none being allowed to be taught there by the rules'.[31]

In October 1845, Mrs Smith was again complaining. She advised one of the Board's inspectors about a hedge-school in Weaver's Square adjoining her estate, where the pupils were crowded into a little room 'the size of a pantry and taught by a succession of incompetent masters against whose malpractices he [Father Germaine] never finds one word to say'. This school had existed for some time but Mrs Smith was amazed that another one had just been established by the curate, Father Galvin, who 'professes to assist us yet after his friendly consultation with me he went and set up a hedge-school within a mile, selecting a master for it with the utmost care'. It was at this point that Mrs Smith resolved, with the co-operation of the school inspector, to appeal once more to Dr Murray. A short time later she recorded that Father Germaine had been summoned for a consultation with his bishop and had returned much changed. He wrote her 'the kindest possible note' about which she commented with barely concealed irony, 'we are to walk through the parish hereafter hand in hand doing good and peace ensuing'. But nothing much changed in reality; four years later, she noted in her diary that after almost a decade of non-cooperation, she had come to the conclusion that the local priests 'preferred the hedge-schools as more manageable and less instructive, much learning being in the way of people who had their bread to earn by labour'.[32]

🔖 10 The Famine Years

'The peasant can live...if the crop do not fail.'

SC AND AM HALL

In April 1845, the third marquis was inspecting a remote part of the estate on one of his regular visits to Blessington. Accompanied by William Owen, he left Mr Armstrong's house at Kippure Park, having ridden out from Dublin that morning through the Sallygap. Owen had just left him to ride ahead to alert some of the tenants that the marquis wished to speak to them about improvements to their holdings when, according to a newspaper account, 'he happened to turn around and found the noble marquis prostrate on the ground, the mare walking over him; he hastened to his assistance, and on taking him in his arms inquired if he was hurt; the only reply he received was a slight groan, when his Lordship instantly expired'.[1]

The funeral took place with great ceremony. The body was brought back to Mr Armstrong's house and from there to Dublin. The funeral procession to the north some days later was accompanied by the more notable Blessington tenants. Having passed through Drogheda, it arrived in Newry and from there to Hillsborough. It was everywhere met by the chief residents and tenants of the Downshire northern estate who wore 'mourning garb and a band of crepe on the left arm' as a mark of respect for 'one of the best and most affectionate landlords'.[2] It was estimated that at one stage upwards of 3,000 people accompanied the cortege, '2,000 walking, 400 on horseback, 300 in gigs and 150 in private carriages'.

78 *Funeral of the third marquis*

The marquis's body lay in state overnight in the drawing room at Hillsborough Castle and the following morning, before the burial in the family vault at Hillsborough, the new marquis appeared at the gates of the castle and gave orders that 'such of the tenantry as were anxious to see the coffin should be admitted'. Many of those present did so and a local newspaper account describes the scene. The coffin was covered with crimson velvet and surmounted with gilt escutcheons and a plate on which were displayed the coronet and crest, titles, name and age of the dead marquis. The room was hung with black, the windows were closed, and at each side of the coffin large wax tapers were burning; 'many aged and infirm men were present and seemed much affected'.[3]

Despite a lifetime's endeavour, the third marquis had not found a solution to the financial difficulties of the estate, and at the time of his death the debt was in the region of £400,000, a £100,000 increase on that which he had inherited. His demise was but a prelude to a greater tragedy, which a few short months later would engulf the country.

The population of Ireland in 1800 was estimated at about five million; by 1821 the figure had run to six and a half million; by 1841 it had risen to eight million. The Halls, who visited Ireland several times before the Great Famine, blamed the potato, which had been introduced at the end of the sixteenth century. They noted that 'a very limited portion of land, a few days of labour and a small amount of manure will create a stock upon which a family may live for twelve months...nearly every soil will produce potatoes'.[4] This availability of food led to the subdivision of land in many areas. Sons and daughters could throw up a cabin, sow their potatoes and rear a family, which would in turn repeat the process. 'The peasant can live,' summed up the Halls, '*if the crop do not fail.*' But it did fail. During the thirty years preceding the Great Famine there had been several 'minor' famines, usually accompanied by an outbreak of fever such as typhus or cholera. And the Halls were not correct in assuming that a family could live for twelve months on their potatoes; there was always a period of about three months between the end of one crop and the harvesting of the next when thousands of labourers were forced to migrate in search of work, leaving their families with no alternative but to beg. In times of famine this trend was exacerbated. The partial failures of the potato crop in the years 1816-7, 1822-3 and 1830-1 were a portent of the catastrophe facing the country should a general failure occur, leading to a warning by a Dublin physician, Dominick Corrigan, that unless the people were provided with an alternative source of food, sooner or later a general failure of the potato would bring about pestilence and disease of unprecedented magnitude.

The Government was not entirely inactive. Between 1800 and 1840, it had set up a number of major commissions to investigate endemic poverty in Ireland and one of these, the Poor Inquiry Commission, reported that almost two and a half million people were 'in such a state of poverty as to require organised welfare schemes'. In England a poor rate or local tax on property to pay for the destitute of each parish had been introduced under the Tudors in the sixteenth century. This was the origin of the English Poor Law, which in 1834 was radically amended. Relief from now on was only to be given in workhouses, which were administered by Boards of Guardians, elected by the ratepayers of a certified union of parishes. The Poor Law rates provided the finance. In 1838 the Government introduced a similar Poor Law into Ireland but for various reasons it was unsuitable. A system which had been designed for one of the most advanced economies of its time could not easily be transferred to Ireland with its enormous problems of poverty. The scheme was initially opposed by people from opposite ends of the political spectrum, such as Lord Castlereagh and Daniel O'Connell (the latter eventually supported the bill). The Churches were also unhappy, particularly at the institutionalised nature of the workhouses, and most landlords were hostile but none of the scheme's critics could 'exert themselves sufficiently to prevent its adoption'.[5] And so the Poor Law 'for the effective relief of the destitute poor in Ireland' was passed. The country was divided into 130 districts or unions, each with its own workhouse, run by Boards of Guardians, which became responsible for the support of the destitute poor of the area. The principle that 'the property of Ireland will pay for the poverty of Ireland' through the Poor Rate was put in place and the first workhouse opened in 1840.[6]

In 1845 the potato crop was attacked by blight. The disease struck with lightning rapidity. 'I can recall precisely the day, almost the hour, when the blight fell on the potatoes,' recorded Frances Power Cobbe in county Dublin. 'A party of us were driving to a seven o'clock dinner at the house of our neighbour. As we passed a remarkably fine field of potatoes in blossom, the scent came through the open windows of the carriage, and we remarked how splendid the crop. Three or four hours later, as we returned home in the dark, a dreadful smell came from the same field, and we exclaimed, "Something has happened to those potatoes; they do not smell at all as they did when we passed them on our way out."'[7]

Robert Peel, the Prime Minister in 1845, responded quickly and effectively in the first year. To keep the price of food within the means of those in need, American maize was sold cheaply, local voluntary committees made up of landlords and the middle classes were set up to organise the distribution of food, and public works to provide employment were initiated. But his government was replaced in June 1846 by a liberal or Whig administration,

79 A soup kitchen

and the Head of the Treasury with responsibility for famine relief was Charles Trevelyan. He was an advocate of the prevailing *laissez-faire* philosophy which stressed the virtue of private enterprise, and believed that the people 'would never resort to honest industry and become self-sufficient if they were provided with free handouts of food at government expense'. Disaster followed. It is estimated that during the six years between 1845 and 1851 the population of the country decreased by two million; something like a million people died of starvation and disease and the rest fled the country, carrying with them a legacy of bitterness and hate which was later to foment rebellion.[8]

80   The death cart

The most immediate short-term effect of the Famine on the estate system was to hasten existing trends. During those six years smallholdings of one to five acres declined by at least half, and the process of consolidation was speeded up with an increase in the number of holdings of over 30 acres. The latter process was accelerated by the infamous 'Gregory clause' contained in an Act of June 1847, which decreed that any person who occupied more than a quarter of a statute acre and who applied for a place in the workhouse or food for his family had to give up his patch of land.[9] After thousands of deaths, however, the Poor Law Commissioners relented and agreed that the 'quarter acre' men could be helped.

Although no part of Ireland escaped the ravages of the Famine, its effects were more keenly felt in some areas than in others, particularly in the heavily populated marginalised areas in the west. In general Wicklow was not badly hit. One reason was that Dublin, with opportunities for non-agricultural employment, was little more than thirty kilometres away. One historian has stated that 'in no other part of Ireland was there such a high rate of inter-county migration as there was between Wicklow and Dublin'.[10] It is estimated that about one-seventh of the people born in Wicklow were living in Dublin in the 1840s; by the early 1850s this had increased to one-fifth. Another reason was that the Blessington estate had been well managed for the previous thirty years. The third marquis kept in constant touch with his agents and the fact that these agents were resident ensured an official presence in the area. William Owen, the agent during the Famine years, made contributions on his own and on the marquis's behalf to the local relief committee and kept a watch on the condition of the tenants.

As early as April 1846, the Smiths at Baltiboys were concerned about 'the miseries of our poor' and had bought maize to sell at low cost to them. The maize mixed with potatoes would help, they hoped, 'keep our own people in comfort through these always scarce months'. A month later Mrs Smith recounted an incident that affected her deeply. While picnicking at Blackamore hill, over Lacken, 'a little frightened boy, the herd of some cattle grazing on these uplands', had collected the 'shakings' from their tablecloth. With crusts of bread in one hand he gnawed at bare bones held in the other and was 'the impersonation of famine'.[11]

By the autumn alarms bells were ringing. It was possible for people to survive one bad harvest but when the blight returned for a second year and destroyed what at first appeared a bumper crop, a real calamity was at hand. Government officials estimated that about 30 per cent of the potato crop in the Blessington area was affected and in September a meeting of the neighbouring gentry took place to consider the state of the starving poor.[12] A crowd of 'two or three hundred' people gathered in the town, anxious 'to know that they would be looked after,' and in October, a relief committee with the Earl of Milltown in the chair was set up, and a subscription fund established to buy provisions; the marquis gave £20, the Earl of Milltown and George Joy, an absentee landlord with lands in Lacken, gave £10, John Finnemore, the Hornidge brothers and Colonel Smith, £5 each, Rev Ogle Moore £3, and Rev Arthur Germaine, the parish priest of Hollywood and Lacken £2.[13] The secretary, Ogle Moore, wrote in November 1846 to the central relief committee in Dublin seeking employment for about 100 destitute people in the area, and on Christmas Eve, when a heavy fall of snow covered the countryside, he reported that 'there was not four days' supply of provisions in the town' and what little flour and oatmeal was available was 'bad and dear'.[14] The marquis acknowledged the hardship being felt and granted the tenants a reduction on the half-year rent which had

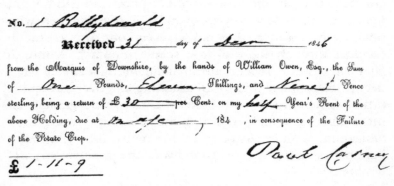

81 Receipt for rent reduction in 1846

been due in November. Both large and smallholders benefited from this reduction, which varied between five and fifty per cent, with the higher figure generally granted to smallholders.[15] He also initiated relief work, mainly improving the roads, as a means of support to the most destitute. Although work commenced that November most was undertaken between May 1847 and December 1848. A few of the more substantial tenants were engaged by William Owen to supervise the work. Carbery Healy, a tenant from Oldcourt, was responsible for supervising road works at Threecastles, Ballyward, Oldcourt and Blackrock, while work at Woodend and on the bog road to Sorrell Hill as well as a 'new road through Knockieran and Rathnabo' was looked after by Andrew Nowlan of Knockieran. Other work undertaken included drainage at Haylands and a bridge at Ballynabrocky.[16] The amount expended on wages varied from week to week. In November 1846 and in May 1847, a sum in excess of £5 per week was spent but we do not know how many people were employed; at other times, especially during the summer months, the amount dropped to around £2 per week.

A good indication of the level of distress caused by the Famine in the Blessington estate can be gauged from the rentals. During the first two years things did not go too badly. The half-yearly rent due from the estate in May 1845 was £3,197, but almost £200 extra was collected due to arrears paid by some of the tenants. In May 1846 and 1847, the agent collected £3,109 and £3,075 respectively, which was more or less the rent due. However, by May 1848 only £2,706 was collected and in May 1849 the figure had dropped to £2,534. Six months later the November rents only brought in £2,240. A growing number of tenants could not pay and at the end of 1849 the number of defaulters reached a peak. The larger tenants were better able to pay their rents in full throughout the years of the Famine but an exception was George Tassie of Threecastles, who farmed 200 acres and whose family had

TOWNLAND AND TENANT	Quantities by Surveys	Arrears Remaining 1 May 1849	Half Year's Rent Due 1 Nov 1849	Poor Rate Allowed	Received by Mr Owen	Arrears Remaining 1 Nov 1849	OBSERVATIONS
Ballylow							
1 John Fitzsimons	4 2 26	16 16	3 2		3 2	18 18 9	Notice to Quit served.
2 Widow Purcell	4 2 26	11 18 9	2 2			13 8 9	leave.
3 Andrew McEvoy	4 2 25	5 2	1 10	3 10		47 2	Pay from family of Widow Welsh
4 Peter Moran	13 3 36	6 16 1	7 17	3 1		76 8 1	Notice to Quit served
5 Bryan Sheridan	13 3 36	13 16	9 12			13 16	
6 John G. L.	6 3 38	19 18 8	4 12		4 12	23 16 8	Notice to Quit served
7 Edward Lawler	6 3 38	46	4	10		57 10	Pay from but Dept Arrears
8 Robt Fitzsimmons	13 3 35	36 15	11 10	3 2	12 5	36 18	Notice to Quit served
9 Edward Carney	13 3 35	4 10	12 5		4 10	4 10	Notice to Quit served
10 John Brady	6 3 38	77 8 3	4 10			81 8 3	+ Notice to Quit served
11 Widow Brady	6 3 28		4				
12 Mountain	1676 26						
	1677 3 35	333 1 9	65	17 1	24 9	373 12 9	

been associated with stone quarrying in nearby Golden Hill. He was unable to pay his rent in 1845 – a temporary aberration the agent hoped – but he continued to default and by 1848 he had given up his holding. The smaller tenants, particularly in the marginalised upland areas of Ballynatona, Ballydonnell, Ballynasculloge and Ballylow, experienced considerable difficulties, although many did survive and remained on the estate.[17]

The worst hit townland was Ballylow and it was here that most of the evictions on the estate occurred. Many of the tenants were in arrears of rent in 1849 and had been 'noticed to quit' but no action was taken. In Ballylow, however, evictions did take place and the most vulnerable were cleared off the estate. By 1852 nine of the eleven tenants, including a 'very poor family of orphan children', had disappeared from the records, leaving only two families, John and Robert Fitzsimons, on their small-holdings. Two years later, Robert, a 'very poor but respectable tenant' gave up 'possession', leaving only John in Ballylow where his descendants retained a holding until the end of the century.[18] There is some evidence to indicate that a deliberate decision was taken to clear this part of the estate in order to build a shooting lodge, the ruins of which can be seen today beside the remains of the tenants' former homes on the side of the mountain.

Another indication of the impact of the Famine is population decline. In Blessington, the overall population of the estate decreased from 1,969 people in 1841 to 1,384 in 1851, a loss of almost 30 per cent. Apart from Ballylow, the parts of the estate most affected were Knockieran, Ballydonnell, Threecastles and Oldcourt. That in Knockieran Lower dropped from 124 to 50 people; in Ballydonnell North and South from 86 to 36; in Three-castles from 148 to 85 persons; and in Oldcourt from 362 to 243, all above the average decrease.

In general the population loss on the estate was due to the disappearance of smallholders and cottiers. But while the smallholders, who held about five acres each, were always a vulnerable group, the cottiers and labourers were even more at risk, as they were usually landless and dependent on casual work. They did not appear as tenants on the rent books but lived on the fringes of the estate and indeed of society. They were in fact the silent majority that disappeared during the Famine and its aftermath, without a voice being raised.

On the Blessington estate, Oldcourt was the townland with the largest number of cottiers and labourers. When the third marquis successfully regained possession of the leased holdings in the 1840s, the land had already been subdivided and settled by landless cottiers. In 1841, fifty-four houses were clustered in Oldcourt, many of which were probably no more than cabins at the side of the road, but only twenty tenants were officially listed in the estate rental. In other words, thirty-four households in Oldcourt lived at subsistence level, either earning a few pence as casual labourers for the larger farmers or living totally on the potato crop from a tiny plot of land. During the period 1841 to 1851 eighteen of these households, a total of 119 people, disappeared without trace.[19] In nearby Three-castles, the situation was not dissimilar; of the twenty-one houses recorded in the townland in 1841, only eleven belonged to official tenants of the estate. The remainder were landless cottiers, and of the 148 persons living there in 1841, sixty-three had disappeared by 1851.

One reason for the existence of so many landless cottiers in these two townlands was probably the extensive quarrying in both areas; by the nineteenth century this had ceased but the labouring class remained on in deteriorating conditions. Two other townlands that suffered significant population loss were Ballydonnell North and South, in one of the most remote areas of the estate. The 1851 census shows that fifty people had disappeared, leaving only a fraction of the previous population.[20]

Tenants who gave up their holdings peacefully were often

compensated, but in Ballylow only three of the nine evicted tenants appear to have been given compensation. Such was their poverty that the only possession considered worthy of recompense was manure from their black cattle; for this £2 was paid to Bryan Sheridan, £4 10s to John Brady and £5 to Robert Fitzsimons. The occupants of a few huts on the widow McDaniel's 32-acre holding in Knockieran were given 15s, and the widow Farrell received £3 compensation for her 1-acre holding in the same townland. The better-off tenants got more substantial payments. George Dall with 87 acres in Blackrock, and Martin Keogh with 53 acres in Knockieran Lower, were given £30 and £40 11s respectively to assist them to emigrate, while George Tassie of Threecastles received £170 for improvements made to his holding and an annuity of £50 on which he was able to retire to the town.

The custom of buying out tenants furthered the process of consolidation. In Knockieran Lower, four of the surviving tenants increased their lands by between five and 14 acres, while in Threecastles two new tenants, who had no previous association with the estate, benefited from the redistribution of Tassie's land and that of three other tenants. John Kinsella, the newly appointed agriculturist to the estate, acquired 48 acres, and Christopher Shepherd, 176 acres. The latter also obtained another large farm from a neighbouring landowner, Ogle Moore in Kilbride.

Where did the dispossessed cottiers, labourers and small tenants go? Some probably migrated to Dublin while others found their way to the workhouse in Naas.[21] When first established the workhouses were seen as hateful institutions, a last resort for the very destitute. By late 1846 the numbers seeking admittance to workhouses rose dramatically. Naas became grossly overcrowded, with numbers peaking in the winters of 1847 and 1848; according to tradition, many came from the northern part of West Wicklow, which included Blessington.[22] In January 1847, the Board of Guardians was urgently looking for additional space to augment the original 550 places; a house was hired to accommodate 100 inmates and stables were fitted up for an additional 50, while a new fever ward provided 44 places.

Although hunger and disease accounted for much of the loss of population during the Famine years, emigration was also a major factor, a process assisted by some landlords who wanted to clear their estates and be relieved of paying the Poor Rates on small holdings valued at below £4. The Marquis of Lansdowne's agent argued that it would be cheaper for the landlord and better for the 3,000 smallholders on his estate near Kenmare if a once-off payment of about £14,000 was made 'for their emigration at once, than to continue to support them at home'.[23] On the Coolattin estate in south Wicklow, Lord Fitzwillian's agent arranged for 300 families, amounting to 1,600 people, to leave the country, 'cabins to be thrown down' whether the people agreed to go or not.[24] Such schemes were not highly significant in the overall picture of emigration at the time, and did not occur on the Blessington estate, where the tenants who emigrated mostly did so by using whatever resources they could lay their hands on. A few were assisted by the Downshires – the Carney family from Ballydonnell were given sums ranging from £6 10s to £20 12s 6d. Paul and Tim Carney left for America in 1848, Maurice went the year after and Anthony

83 Cabins with roofs stripped off

followed in 1850, leaving two other members of the family, Edward and Peter, behind.

Compared to some other parts of the country, the Blessington area escaped the worst effects of the Famine. Elizabeth Smith, nonetheless, refers to a statement in the House of Commons in 1847 that many people were starving in Talbotstown Lower, the barony in which the estate was located. The fourth marquis apparently was so concerned about this that he decided to come to Blessington to see for himself. His visit assured him that the remarks in the Commons did not refer to his own estate but to the area beyond Hollywood owned by Lord Beresford, which according to Mrs Smith was a 'wretched den for pauper squatters'.[25] She was equally critical of some other absentee landlords in the area like the Radcliffes and Vavasours.

Mrs Smith visited her tenants systematically during the Famine, and provided daily for the most needy – upwards of 22 in 1847. At the height of the Famine she visited Judy Doyle, the former nurse of one of the Smith children, and found her living in the most awful squalor, four almost naked children squatting on the floor of a small kitchen bereft of furniture except for a 'crazy dresser' with little upon its shelves, while the only bedroom was used to house two cows. Notwithstanding the dreadful living conditions, the family was not destitute, having eight barrels of oats besides the cows, highlighting the fact that bad living conditions did not always reflect acute want.[26]

Although the Famine petered out in 1850, its effects were catastrophic, not only for the people but also for the landowners. Encumbered with debts, faced with falling rents and the added financial burden of the Poor Law, the seeds were sown for the demise of the landlord system.

🪶 11 The Social Round

*'Peers and gentles going down, down, down,
never to rise again.'*

ELIZABETH SMITH

In 1845 the fourth Marquis of Downshire, Arthur Wills
Blundell Sandys Trumbull, the first head of the family to be
born at Hillsborough since the early eighteenth century, 'a
great hulk of a man weighing sixteen stone', inherited the
estate at the age of thirty-three.[1] His coming of age in 1833
and his marriage four years later to a daughter of Lord
Combermere were both celebrated at Hillsborough with a
feast for the tenants. Four thousand people were said to
have sat down at the marriage feast to eat oxen and sheep
roasted on open fires and to drink free beer and whiskey.[2]

He and his wife visited the Blessington estate on a regular
basis, spending about two months each autumn in the latter
part of the 1840s. Their visits were described by Elizabeth
Smith as a boom to the area; 'a sort of energy seems given
by their presence' and 'a deal of money is circulated by the
requirements of the family'. Unlike his father, the fourth
marquis was easy and affable and he and his wife entered
into the social life of the neighbourhood which usually
included a visit to Mrs Smith. On meeting him for the first
time, her acerbic Scottish mind noted that behind his
'charming unaffected manners' he was 'rather stupid'. In
time, however, she revised this opinion and later described
him and his wife as 'truly rational people, full of kind
feelings and totally without affectation'. He stayed for lunch
when he called on her and she was charmed when he helped
in serving the dishes and 'made fun of the want of a

servant'. Likewise, his wife put on few airs and spent many hours riding, driving or walking in all weathers, and delighting the locals by jumping over stiles and ditches and 'facing the hills in her plain shawl and good thick boots'. It was a style of behaviour 'new to Ireland' among the upper class at the time.[3]

The Downshires were so pleased with their Blessington visits that they expressed an interest in spending more time there. They discussed with their neighbours the possibility of building a small cottage on the demesne land or alternatively reconstructing one of the houses in the town but this plan never materialised. The rustic idyll of Blessington life contrasted with the 'regal state' in which they lived in Hillsborough Castle when they visited their northern estate. There, the many guests were waited on by innumerable servants who glided about 'silent as the grave' making sure that nobody wanted for anything.[4] Lavish entertainments were laid on to amuse the guests, which included plays and concerts as well as balls.

84 Contemporary sketch of high society

Despite the Famine life for the gentry and the larger farmers in Blessington went on as before, with little disruption to the social events of their year. This may seem incongruous but it probably underlines the fact that the estate did not suffer the ravages experienced in other parts of the country. The annual ploughing competition went ahead in 1846 and was attended by 'upwards of sixty ploughs' and 'an immense concourse of people, almost everyone in the country, high and low'. The event was followed by a reception, funded by the marquis, for the larger tenants. In October 1847 Mrs Smith and William Owen organised a picnic to nearby Glenbride. While the men 'shot over the moors', the ladies 'tried to reach the source of the Kings river' and in the attempt got so wet that they had 'about an hour's fun drying themselves at different fires', and were forced to dress 'in any stray dry garments at hand'. The day finished with tea for all at Baltiboys House, where the company 'danced till near midnight'.[5]

The following year, Elizabeth and her family with about forty gentry, 'besides the mob', attended the laying of the first stone at a bridge on the upper reaches of the Liffey, where until then a dangerous ford had claimed the lives of many. Lady Downshire laid the foundation stone with a silver trowel presented to her on a silk cushion by Mr Armstrong of Kippure House who had organised the event. The crowd responded enthusiastically with 'deafening' hurrahs, four horns played 'God Save the Queen', Mr Armstrong read a speech to which the marquis replied, and finally the horns concluded the official proceedings with 'See the Conquering Hero'. The gentry were escorted to Kippure House by the horn players who now played the 'March in Figaro', 'Away to the Mountain's Brow' and 'Home Sweet Home'. When they arrived there, 'sheep, well-belled' met them on the lawn where a 'very well got up' banquet was laid on. This was followed by a singsong and later everyone adjourned to the barn where all, high and low, mixed in the dance.[6]

One of the biggest social events of the decade took place in the late summer of 1849, to celebrate the thirty-seventh birthday of the marquis. He wrote beforehand to his friend,

85 Arthur Hill, fourth Marquis of Downshire

Dr Robinson, in Blessington, 'begging of him to help with the preparations' for the supper and ball. 'The whole country is astir,' enthused Mrs Smith, 'and in truth this good landlord is much beloved and well worthy of every mark of respect from his people and indeed from his neighbours, for no man could be more really good-natured.' Her servants went into Blessington some days ahead of the visit to view the preparations. On the arrival of the marquis who was accompanied by his wife, children, servants, governess and secretary, not to mention all their 'appurtenances', the tenants, 'three hundred in number' on horse and on foot, met the cavalcade at Hempstown on the boundary of the estate and escorted it into the village, which was 'illuminated from one end to the other'.[7]

Mrs Smith and her daughters made the customary social call on the Downshires shortly after their arrival. She found the marchioness 'looking very pretty, and she was very affable, quite kind in her manner'. The marquis's genial manner impressed her but the children were dismissed as 'two very ugly boys but rather a nice-looking little girl, tall of her age'. Some days later the marquis called on Mrs Smith at Baltiboys and invited her to lunch on 'a haunch of venison' the following day. He was in no hurry to leave and 'stood gossiping a good half hour'. But the lunch was not totally to Elizabeth's satisfaction; although she was impressed by the manner in which they were served, the cook showed little culinary skill, the entertainment was 'stupid enough', and 'there was no musick, no cards and the room is very small'. In addition, 'my Lady has not much to say', although 'my Lord chatters away at a great rate and very pleasantly'. He was full of the ball and hoped the Smiths would honour the event with their presence. Meanwhile in the old inn preparations were going ahead; four bullocks, twenty sheep, lambs, hams and five-hundred weight of plum pudding were being prepared days in advance 'under the charge of an old messman' who was paid a guinea a day for his services.[8]

Although all social classes attended the ball on 6 August, they were strictly segregated. Among the local gentry, the 'elite of the company' were Elizabeth Smith and her family, the Tyntes of Dunlavin, the Hornidges of Tulfarris, as well as the larger farmers of the area, such as the Darkers, Boothmans, Kilbees and Merreys. These 'selects' dined in five upstairs rooms of the old hotel, while three rooms on the ground floor were put aside for 'the second rank' of people. 'All the mountaineers', presumably the tenants from the uplands of the estate, ate in the 'vaults', and the labouring classes in the schoolhouse. In all, approximately 'one thousand five hundred tenantry and peasantry' dined. The gentlemen of the neighbourhood kept order in the hotel, 'carved for the awkward and served drink'. Afterwards the tables were cleared and dancing took place in all the rooms, 'pipers and fluters being plenty'. The ball was opened by a country-dance, and Janey Smith, Elizabeth's daughter, was the centre of attraction,

86 *Contemporary sketch of country ball*

partnering the marquis, while the marquis's brother, Lord
Sandys, danced with Mrs Tynte of Dunlavin. The
marchioness, who looked 'like an angel' in her white dress,
also took part in the dancing until, finally exhausted, she
was escorted by John Hornidge and Mr Wolfe to the agent's
house 'where she went at once to bed'. Dancing also took
place in every 'publick house' in the town, and in the
Market House 'Kavanagh's Band played excellent musick',
while in the square outside 'an immense crowd' gathered
about a bonfire. The tenants, especially the 'mountaineers'
were in high humour and at one stage mistaking Mrs Smith
and her husband for the marquis and marchioness 'cheered
us lustily to our great entertainment'.

The weather, however, did not co-operate and Mrs
Smith recounted that the rain prevented much of 'the fun
we selects had promised ourselves', being unable to move
freely from one place of amusement to another. It also
meant that the 'mob' outside, growing 'unmannerly', would
have forced their way into the hotel had they not been
restrained by 'gentlemen' and 'yeomen' stationed at the
door. The hospitality was such that 'long before midnight
there was hardly a sober man' in the town. Some of 'the

incapables' were put to bed, while others spent the night in the police barracks. But all ended well; the incapables 'got off unreprimanded' and Mrs Smith remarked that sometimes it was 'judicious' for those in authority to be blind and deaf to the excesses of the lower orders.

The ball provided a rich topic of conversation for Mrs Smith and her friends who over the following days discussed 'the dress of the mountain ladies, the manners of the mountain gentleman and such matters'. But she was somewhat piqued by the overlap of the Blessington ball with a national event – the visit of Queen Victoria to Ireland from 3 to 12 August. 'Our party was hurt by the Queen,' she declared, 'so many had gone in to see her enter Dublin.'

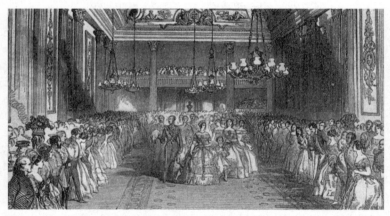

87   Queen Victoria at Dublin Castle

The newspaper reports, to her chagrin, also focussed on the queen – 'our fête is slightly alluded to in the *Mail* today, the Queen fills the paper'.[9]

Some weeks later, another ball in honour of the Downshires was organised by two of the local 'bachelours', Dick Hornidge and Dr Robinson. The assistance of the Smiths was sought and every room at Baltiboys House was engaged for the occasion with some of the guests staying overnight. The night itself 'was admirably managed and went off in high style' with Lady Downshire and John Hornidge of Tulfarris opening the ball. Lady Downshire, who danced all night, 'was splendidly dressed' in 'Brussels lace over pink satin, a string of pearls round her head, lappets at the back'. Mrs Smith particularly noted the necklace – 'four rows of large pearls fastened in front by a quantity of fine diamonds nearly covering the neck'. Everybody 'was in good humour' and the 'lights, musick, refreshments, supper, company' all were 'superlative'.[10]

Shooting parties were also the order of the day. A four-day event was organised by Mr Shehan, the editor of the *Dublin Evening Mail*, who owned a lodge at Kilbeg, near Lacken. As a result Mrs Smith declared that her larder was full and that 'we are living on game'. Before the Downshires left, towards the end of the second week in September, the marchioness paid a visit to Mrs Smith to return 'the plate and other things she had borrowed of us'. Elizabeth was impressed by her conscientiousness; 'like any other honest man's wife' she had kept a list of the borrowed items 'and was in a fidget about a fork of Mrs Finnemore's' which she had thought had 'gone astray'.[11]

During the Downshire visit of 1849 there was no mention of the tragedy that was happening in the country generally; it was as if the horrors of the Famine and the widespread destitution did not exist. But with the departure of the Downshires, the problems of the contemporary scene – the recurrence of blight in some areas, the increasing inability of the tenants to pay rents, the burden of the Poor Law and the indebtedness of the landlord class, which for a few short weeks had been forgotten – once again became the chief concern of Mrs Smith. To her astute mind, one thing was now becoming obvious; a change was at hand which would have serious implications for her own class. In February 1850, when the Famine was ending, she wrote the following prophetic words in her diary: 'Peers and gentles going down, down, down, never to rise again'.[12]

12 The Final Chapter

'I feel confident that we shall kill the Irish landlord system.'

CHARLES STEWART PARNELL

The Great Famine was the death knell for numerous landlords. By 1849 the Government was forced to pass legislation – the Encumbered Estates Act – by which creditors could force the sale of estates that were heavily in debt. Over five million acres valued at twenty million pounds changed hands, either to solvent landlords or local speculators.[1] It was not enough, however, to alter the pattern of land ownership; over 80 per cent of holdings were still held in units in excess of 1,000 acres.

The 1850s and 1870s were on the whole characterised by a recovery in agriculture, very evident in dairying areas due in the main to a dramatic increase in the price of butter and store cattle. The recovery was helped by the expansion of the railroads, which allowed easier access to markets.[2] Evictions and clearances became less usual after 1854 and many tenants, although not those in the marginalised areas, became more prosperous. But despite the efforts at consolidation, farms of between 15 and 30 acres predominated.

One notable development was an increase in land held in 'conacre'; middle to large-sized holdings which became available were no longer leased but let to the highest bidder for an eleven-month period. Letting in this manner benefited the landlords as the tenants had no claim to continued occupancy and there was less difficulty in collecting rents. Thus despite the fact that rents, the main source of the landowner's income, did not increase

168

significantly, some landlords prospered during this time. Many got involved in farming themselves, utilising demesne land for this purpose. Lord Clonbrock of Galway and Willoughby Bond of Longford became substantial farmers in their own right, as did the de Robeck family, who built a house on their estate near Ballymore Eustace.[3]

On the Blessington estate, the fourth marquis, like his father before him, was committed to encouraging good agricultural practices and continued to invest in improvements. Turnip seed for the tenants was purchased from a Dublin firm and the estate undertook the expense of keeping four bulls, four rams and two boars for breeding purposes. Later a stallion was added to the stock and 115 sheep at a cost of £226 4s were distributed among the tenants. Thomas Cullen, a tenant with 52 acres in Hempstown, was given ten ewes and a ram at a cost to the estate of £13 5s. A full-time agriculturalist was added to the permanent estate staff and a nursery encouraged the planting of trees. The annual ploughing competition continued to take place, and a new development was the starting of a horticultural society by the marchioness.[4] Her 'intended flower show and premiums', according to Elizabeth Smith, 'have spirited up her neighbours', and when the event took place, in September 1850, it was deemed to have been 'wonderfully fair for a first attempt'. To Mrs Smith's delight, three prizes were won by 'our Darkers' – her steward's family and the premier tenants on her estate.[5] The marchioness also promoted the making of local frieze cloth in the upland townlands and subsequently bought the products. John Fitzsimons and Margaret Murphy were paid £9 15s and £6 19s 6d respectively for one hundred yards of frieze for clothing for labouring men on the estate and cloth was also sent to Hillsborough.[6]

In all, the marquis was reported to have expended upwards of £20,000 on maintenance and improvements and on allowances to tenants on the estate during the period 1845 to 1868.[7] This included arrears of about

£8,000 that had been written off on his instruction (as many of these had been outstanding for decades there was little likelihood of their ever being honoured). In 1861, at the request of the fourth marquis, the Dublin firm of Brassington and Gale surveyed and revalued the estate and advised an increase of 20 per cent. But the Hillsborough administration decided on a much smaller increase – five per cent on the 1845 rent, which was well below the average in the country generally.

In 1868, the fourth marquis died suddenly at the age of fifty-six. He was succeeded by his son, who visited Blessington with his wife in October 1870, where a fireworks display took place and porter was distributed to the tenants.[8] But the reign of the fifth marquis was brief; he died at the age of twenty-nine in 1874. A long minority then ensued, during which time the estate was managed by three trustees – Lord Bridport, Colonel Bateson and Lord Arthur Hill, the younger brother of the fifth marquis.[9] The sixth marquis finally inherited in 1892 and although Lord Arthur Hill maintained strong links with the northern estate, staying regularly at Hillsborough Castle and serving for nearly thirty years as MP for county Down, the close connection between the Downshires and Blessington had already ended with the death of the fourth marquis twenty-four years earlier.

Two major issues dominated post-Famine Ireland – land reform and self-government. The latter movement had two strands. The first was epitomised by parliamentarians like Isaac Butt, Charles Stewart Parnell and John Redmond, whose political aims were pursued through the Westminster Parliament where the Irish MPs formed a powerful and influential block. The other strand – the Young Irelanders and the Fenians – was revolutionary.

The Young Ireland movement was founded in the early 1840s by Thomas Davis, Charles Gavin Duffy and John Blake Dillon, middle-class intellectuals. They advocated non-sectarian nationalism and used their newspaper, *The Nation,* to inform public opinion. Later, more revolutionary members, like John Mitchel, advocated rebellion but after an ill-fated rising in 1848, which ended with the deportation of its leaders, the movement collapsed.

The Fenians, who originated in America, where they found ready support among emigrants and supporters of the Young Irelanders, planned an uprising in 1867. It failed and many of its leaders were imprisoned. But the Fenian movement did not disappear; it went underground, and retained support both in Ireland and America to keep alive the nationalist ideals that were to reappear in Easter 1916.

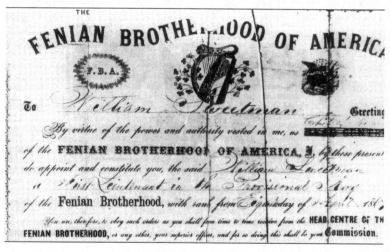

88 Fenian membership card

Land reform was the second big issue in the latter half of the nineteenth century. With the extension of the franchise in 1850, which significantly increased the number of people eligible to vote, the balance of power in the country began to shift. Long before the secret ballot became law in 1872, Irish voters had begun to resist landlord pressure and increasingly put nationalist candidates into the Westminster Parliament. By now there was an awareness of the 'Irish question' among politicians and statesmen in England, intensifying when William Gladstone, the leader of the Liberal Party, became Prime Minister. His aims for Ireland were the disestablishment of the Church of Ireland, the extension of university education to Catholics, and above all land reform. He championed the Land Acts of 1870 and 1881, which paved the way for the tenants to become the proprietors of their land. Although the act of 1870 gave some measure of tenant protection and established the right of tenants to buy out their holdings, in practice the former often proved difficult to define in law and the latter only became a reality with the passing of the act of 1881.

There were three key figures behind the movement for land reform: Charles Stewart Parnell, an MP and Protestant landlord, with an estate at Rathdrum in county Wicklow; Michael Davitt, son of a smallholder who had been evicted from his Mayo farm during the Famine; and the Fenian, John Devoy, forced into exile in America after the 1867 rising. They met in Dublin in June 1879, where they worked out an agreement that became known as the New Departure. This was an acceptance that there was a fundamental link between the agrarian struggle and the fight for independence, an idea first mooted in the writings of James Fintan Lawlor in the aftermath of the Famine; he had argued that the land would become the engine that would drive the national question in its train. The New Departure cemented the link.

The late 1870s were years of hardship. A series of bad harvests, coupled with an economic depression in England, meant that the tenants were unable to pay their rents. Food was scarce and the spectre of famine loomed again, especially in the west. Against this background Michael Davitt founded the first Land League branch in August 1879 in his native Mayo, and two months later the organisation had spread countrywide. Its aims were twofold: to organise resistance to the landlords for the immediate purpose of preventing evictions and securing a

89 Meeting of the Land League committee

reduction in rents, and ultimately to transform the tenant farmers into owners of their holdings.[10] The League organisers, with the aid of American funds, now travelled throughout the country to give advice and support to tenants in their legal battles against the landlords and help with money in cases of distress. Parnell exhorted the people to 'hold a firm grip on your homesteads and land' while Davitt raised the clarion call: 'The land of Ireland for the people of Ireland.'

The authorities in Dublin and London were alarmed by the approach adopted by the League. The organisation was now assuming the authority of the Government by convening courts to decide local disputes and to ensure that the Land League rules were being upheld. Mass meetings were held throughout the country demanding a reduction in rents to the level of Griffith's Valuation of 1848-1860. Tenants were encouraged to offer their landlord what they considered a fair rent – on many estates, they sought reductions of upwards of 20 per cent – and payment was withheld if the landlord did not accept.

One result of the economic difficulties and non-payment
of rent was the increase in the number of evictions. The
League tried to prevent these but if they did take place, it
supported the tenants with practical aid and, importantly,
by not allowing anyone else to take the holding or buy the
stock. Large numbers of people attended the evictions,
which got prominent coverage in the newspapers of the day.
In January 1880, the *Kildare Observer* reported that in
Maam in Connemara, 'over 160 police' dispersed a 'large
gathering of peasantry' who were there to protest at the
eviction of eight tenants from their holdings on the Martin
estate; some days later 'a land meeting', presided over by
the parish priest, took place and two Government
'shorthand writers' who were present had to have police
protection to and from Galway. The following month at
Kilcrow, near Athy, the sub-sheriff retreated and did not

90 *Agent fleeing hostile crowd*

91 Captain Boycott thanking his harvesters

proceed with the eviction of a family from their smallholding when he saw the large attendance of League supporters.[11]

One of the most forceful weapons used by the Land League was the social ostracism of landlords or their agents. The most celebrated, which added a new word to the English language, was that of Captain Boycott, Lord Erne's agent in county Mayo. The tenants refused to give assistance in the harvesting of his crops and prevented anyone else from doing so. After a prolonged stand-off, fifty Orange workers from Cavan, guarded by 1,000 policemen, were drafted in to harvest the crops at a cost to the Government of £10,000. The boycott was extended to tenants who had paid their rent while their neighbours were withholding theirs and to those who tendered for land from which others had been evicted. Neighbours broke off all social contact with such people who were treated 'like lepers of old'.[12] Where legal proceedings were taken against tenants, and animals and crops were seized to be sold at 'sheriff sales' to defray arrears of rent, nobody would bid except League representatives who bought back the cattle or produce and restored it to the original tenants (as had happened in the case of Fearis on the Blessington estate over forty years before). In August 1881, a sheriff's sale of cattle for non-payment of rent took place in Baltinglass but according to the *Kildare Observer* only the League put in a bid for the cattle, which 'did not realise the amount of the judgement and cost'.[13] Later the cattle were 'marched in procession through the town, followed by a couple of thousand people'.

Davitt and Parnell advocated peaceful tactics in the pursuit of the aims of the Land League but violence, the legacy of the agrarian secret societies of the past, was never far from the surface. Parnell, who stated that he always 'carefully abstained from recommending others to break the law', advised members of a county Clare branch of the League who were intent on ploughing up the land of neighbouring tenants under notice of eviction that such a gesture was unlawful and ought not be pursued.[14] But throughout the years of the Land War violence often erupted and the maiming of cattle, intimidation, burnings and shootings took place. Landowners, increasingly alarmed at what was happening, formed a Property Defence Association to protect their interests. The passing of Gladstone's Second Land Act in August 1881, which set up a Land Commission to arbitrate a fair rent, went a long way to meet the demands of the tenants but did not receive general acceptance.

The Land League was becoming increasingly militant and the Government decided to take a strong line. In February 1881 Michael Davitt had been arrested; in October, Parnell and other leaders followed him into prison and the Land League was outlawed. There was violent reaction across the country but the impasse was only resolved when the Government agreed to an amendment of the Land Act – the Kilmainham treaty of April 1882 – which extended its terms to tenants in arrears. Parnell and

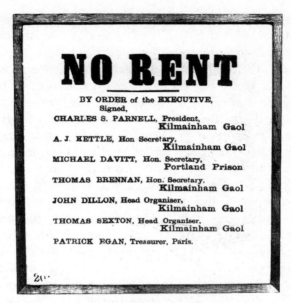

NO RENT

BY ORDER of the EXECUTIVE,
Signed,

CHARLES S. PARNELL, President,
Kilmainham Gaol

A. J. KETTLE, Hon Secretary,
Kilmainham Gaol

MICHAEL DAVITT, Hon. Secretary,
Portland Prison

THOMAS BRENNAN, Hon. Secretary,
Kilmainham Gaol

JOHN DILLON, Head Organiser,
Kilmainham Gaol

THOMAS SEXTON, Head Organiser,
Kilmainham Gaol

PATRICK EGAN, Treasurer, Paris.

92   *'No Rent' poster*

the Land League activists were released from prison in March and April 1882, to be greeted with speechmaking, bonfires, processions, pipe bands and the 'wearing of the green', reflecting the growing feeling of solidarity and power among the people. The release of hotelier Dan Lennon of the Tullow branch from Naas prison was 'the occasion for great celebration'.[15] The ten-kilometer route from the railway station in Carlow town to Tullow was lit by bonfires, and in his home town he was met by two hundred torch-bearers and carried in triumph to the Fair Green where a 'couple of thousand' assembled to celebrate his release.

The first indication of trouble on the Downshire estates occurred in 1880. In the north, the tenants in the mountainous areas around Hilltown in county Down were in a particularly bad way and they sought a reduction of rents. The trustees came on a visit and although no reductions were given, relief was promised to those most affected by the crisis – a ball attended by the dowager marchioness was organised for their benefit.[16]

On the Blessington estate the tenants were suffering similar difficulties but no ball was organised to help them, although that spring the estate bore the cost of seed oats and potatoes for their benefit as did other landowners like Captain Heighington in Donard and Baron de Robeck at Gowran Park.[17] But arrears of rent were mounting and a significant number of tenants, both large and small, were paying only a half-year's rent. Coinciding with the passing of Gladstone's Land Act of August 1881, the tenants formed themselves into an active branch of the Land League and began to agitate. The League was now urging the complete withholding of rents and the Blessington tenants met to review their options. Claiming that they were unable to pay because of the bad harvests, they sought a 25 per cent reduction. The meeting sent a deputation to the agent, William Owen, to tell him of the decision and to offer the reduced rent. Owen refused and the tenants responded by withholding their rents.[18] The Hillsborough administration was now clearly worried: not alone was there a crisis on the Blessington estate, the tenants on the northern estate were also agitating, while at Edenderry a very aggressive campaign against landlordism in general and the Downshires in particular was being orchestrated. By then, Owen had aligned himself with other landlords in the area by joining the Lower Talbotstown branch of the Property Defence Association.[19]

Early in December 1881, Mr Wynn, a senior Downshire official, arrived from England to make an assessment of the situation and to report back to the chief trustee, Viscount Bridport. He visited Owen, who was of the opinion that a 15 per cent allowance should be made on the forthcoming May rents, and also that the November rents, which had not been paid, should have a 'much larger reduction'; he went further and suggested that all the holdings on the estate should be revalued; otherwise 'not a single tenant would come in to pay'. In the light of this, Wynn recommended postponing the new date for collection of the November rents, fixed for later in December, until he had time to discuss the situation with Major McClintock, the chief agent in the north. He then went north and some days later a telegram arrived in Blessington requesting Owen to meet him and McClintock in Dublin to discuss the problem.

At the meeting it was decided to take a hard line and make no concession to the tenants. McClintock thought that a concession would be a tactical mistake, as it would encourage the 'tenants elsewhere to seek a similar reduction'. A reduction of 10 per cent on the important northern rents, would amount to £6,000, a sum almost equal to the entire yearly rents from Blessington. It was felt that it would be preferable to have the Blessington estate 'sink altogether' rather than make such a reduction. Owen was advised to instigate legal proceedings if rents remained unpaid but if any 'loyal' tenants were 'unable to pay their rent on account of distress or want of time' it was his discretion to make reasonable allowances accordingly.[20]

The Blessington tenants refused to back down. According to the *Leinster Leader* they had always had difficulty in paying rents in even 'the most prosperous of years' but in the 'face of the terrible losses of the past seasons and the depression which still weighs down agriculture', payment at this time was 'a physical impossibility'. In common with tenants all over the country, a new determination was evident among them as they continued to withhold their rent, and at a meeting in January 1882, attended by over 130 people, it was 'unanimously resolved to ask for a reduction of 25 per cent'. For a second time a deputation, this time comprising three of the larger Catholic tenants – Patrick Halligan and Hugh Hanlon from Oldcourt and Garret Tallon from Threecastles – were selected to relay the decision to

Owen.[21] He replied that he 'had no authority from the trustees' to grant such a concession and so 'the tenants left in a body without paying any rent'.

Throughout February rumours that Hillsborough was about to take legal action against the Blessington tenants fuelled the rising tension. The *Leinster Leader* declared that 'public sympathy is entirely on the side of the tenants in their struggle for simple justice'. At the same time, the situation on the Edenderry estate, where legal proceedings had been initiated against defaulting tenants, had also come to a head. The *Leinster Leader* sprang to their defence and in ringing tones denounced the Downshires. The official sent from Hillsborough was reported to be 'as solemn as one of Cromwell's roundheads' and behaved as 'if he were the pious Moses Hill, the Provost Marshall of Ulster, who should have quartered on his escutcheon the halter by which he founded the fortunes of a family, when he hanged so many hundreds of the noble O'Neills and O'Donnells of the north'.[22]

Undeterred, Hillsborough decided to act against the Blessington tenants and ejectment decrees were issued. In the past, these decrees were used to put pressure on the tenants to pay but in the majority of cases they were not acted on. Now they would be enforced. Under this kind of pressure, at least one tenant broke ranks and paid his rent in full but as a result he was boycotted and suffered malicious damage to his property.[23] Two of the Oldcourt tenants were first to go. Michael Keogh, a smallholder with seven acres, had been described by Owen four years earlier as 'an improving tenant' and the arrears he then owed were attributed to the loss of some of his cattle; in the intervening years his arrears had increased so that by 1880 they stood at £38, the equivalent of over five years' rent.[24] His eviction in March 1882 was denounced by the Blessington and Oldcourt Ladies' Land League who promised Keogh that they would 'do all they can for him'.[25] Keogh, in fact, was later given back his holding – which was not an unusual occurrence at the time – due to the difficulty of getting another tenant for an 'eviction' farm. The other tenant, Michael Lawler, who had 13 acres and owed £16 or the equivalent of two years rent, died shortly after his eviction and William Lawler, possibly a relation, who at the time held a large farm in the same townland, got his holding.[26]

The cattle of two other tenants in default, Patrick Healy with 18 acres in Haylands and William Freeman with ten acres in the Demesne, were seized in lieu of rent and taken to Blessington to be sold. As with similar sales throughout the country, the occasion turned into a festival. Crowds from adjoining districts thronged the streets, the cattle 'decked in green' were led to the Market Square amid great cheering, and after some bidding the animals were bought back by their former owners. A Ladies' Land League meeting then took place and a former official, T O'Reilly, who had just been released from Naas Jail, was 'given a very popular reception' and 'chaired through the town'.[27]

A week later legal proceedings were taken against a number of the stronger tenants. The three people who had

EVICTION AND RACK-RENT SEIZURES ON THE DOWNSHIRE ESTATE.

DEMONSTRATION IN HONOUR OF A "SUSPECT."

Early on Monday morning a sheriff, bailiff, and some police, went to the house of Michael Keogh Oldcourt, and evicted him. A large number of members of the Ladies' Land League attended, and afterwards proceeded to Blessington to carry out two sales belonging to Patrick Healy and William Freeman. Their cattle were decked in green, and led to the market-square amid great cheering. After some bidding, they were bought in for the tenants; crowds thronged the street from all the surrounding districts, and the

93 Newspaper account of eviction

formed the deputation to Owen the previous January –
Halligan, Hanlon and Tallon – as well as Thomas White of
Oldcourt and James Higgins of Ballynatona were served
notices to attend a sheriff's sale in Bray in early April, where
their holdings were to be sold.[28] They had 'expended a
considerable amount of money reclaiming land and on
permanent buildings' and faced with the prospect of losing
their farms they 'could not see their way to letting their
places' go. So in the end they gave in and agreed to pay.
Many of the other tenants who were withholding rents
followed their example. The ending of the protest in
Blessington coincided with the Kilmainham treaty which
cleared the way for the acceptance of the 1881 act; tenants
in arrears, previously precluded, could now seek a review of
their rent through the newly set up land courts. Economic
conditions improved generally throughout the country and
by the end of the year rents were well paid on the
Blessington estate. It is interesting to note that not all the
tenants on the estate took part in the protest; strong
Protestant farmers in Crosscoolharbour and Threecastles
continued to pay their rent in full.[29]

Gladstone's Second Land Act of 1881 had established
the Irish Land Commission under which rents could be
reviewed by a commissioner and sub-commissioners with
judicial powers. Both tenants and landlords had the right to
appeal this decision. Rents could also be fixed by agreement
between the landlord and tenant and then registered with
the Land Commission. The revised rents were fixed initially
for a period of fifteen years but by 1885, because of the
continuing difficulty experienced by the tenants, a shorter
period of three years was agreed on. Approximately
342,000 cases were dealt with between August 1881 and
December 1902, and average reductions were in the region
of 20 per cent.[30]

By May 1884 twelve of the Blessington tenants,
including those who had been to the forefront in the
agitation two years earlier, had successfully applied for a

94 Land Commission inspecting farmstead

rent review. More tenants applied in the years that followed but the majority waited until the 1890s. The rent reviews in the 1880s generally went to arbitration in the land courts but those in the 1890s were amicably settled by the Downshire administration. Reductions ranged between 6 per cent and 21 per cent. Of the Oldcourt tenants, Patrick Halligan got a 9 per cent reduction, Thomas White over 7 per cent, Michael Keogh and Hugh Hanlon 20 per cent each, and William Freeman and Patrick Healy, the tenants whose cattle had been seized in early 1882, did even better with a 37 per cent reduction. The rent review of the largest and one of the oldest families on the estate, the Finnemores of Ballyward, resulted, however, in an increase of almost 17 per cent – from £154 to £180.[31]

The act of 1881 extended the purchasing terms for tenants – the Land Commission could now give loans of upwards of 75 per cent of the purchasing price of the holdings. The Ashbourne Act four years later significantly enhanced the terms, allowing tenants the full amount of the purchase money and the rate of repayment was lowered.[32]

Under this act, landowners could now sell outlying portions of their estate while retaining the demesne lands; they could sell to the Government and repurchase on the same terms as the tenants. But the terms were still insufficient to entice the main body of landlords to sell and no change in land ownership occurred in Blessington at this time.

Although the setting up of the Land Commission took the heat out of the countrywide agitation, the land problem was by no means solved. By 1885 the economy had taken another downturn; a bad summer in 1884 and deteriorating prices for cattle brought increasing difficulties for farmers. In November 1885 the collection of rents on the Blessington estate again became a problem and arrears now stood at over £5,000. All areas were affected. In the upland townland of Ballynasculloge, two tenants owed £120 and £150 respectively. Crosscoolharbour arrears were £1,203, the Boothmans owing £517 and the Pantons £340.[33] Owen's report to Hillsborough, in which he advocated that no proceedings be taken against many of the tenants, shows that he was adopting a humane approach, especially where widows were concerned. In three cases, ejectment decrees were not implemented. One was the Devoy holding at Butterhill, where £96 was owing; no action was taken in deference to the tenant's mother, an old woman of over ninety years and 'the widow of the former most excellent and worthy tenant, William Devoy, who died some years since aged 96 years'. The widow Higgins in Ballynatona also remained in possession in spite of arrears of £82, as did the widow McDonald in Knockieran Lower, who owed £55. Although Owen was not sanguine about redeeming the debt of Patrick Deegan in Knockieran Upper, who owed £45, no action was taken because of 'the residence on this holding of the widow of the former tenant, a very helpless but most respectable old woman'. Another case which he felt called 'for much and careful consideration' was that of the widow, Esther Murphy, who had arrears of £95 on her holding at Ballysmuttan. In several other cases, Owen also argued that there were extenuating circumstances. Sheep losses were given as a reason in four cases, while other tenants in arrears were described as 'honest, industrious and improving'. Long association with the estate was another consideration; he was sympathetic towards Boothman, one of the larger farmers, because of the 'particular circumstances of this tenant and his family and their conduct towards this office for two generations'.[34]

The agricultural depression continued through 1886, triggering another wave of agitation throughout the country, with many of the tenants unable to pay even the reduced rents set by the Land Commission. In October the National League, an organisation which had been formed after the suppression of the Land League, initiated a new strategy, the Plan of Campaign, which lasted until 1890. This was confined to approximately 120 estates, mainly in the west and south. Under the Plan of Campaign, all tenants on selected estates were to offer their landlord what they considered a fair rent; if this was not accepted, the money would go into an 'estate fund' and, augmented by money from the National League, would be used for the tenants' support. But they were now faced with landlords who were more determined and a Government that successfully combined coercion with conciliation. By 1890 the campaign had petered out, because of the difficulty of funding it, the disastrous split among Parnell's followers and improving agricultural conditions.[35]

Although Blessington was not affected by the Plan of Campaign, tenants were still in difficulties, with a marked increase in the number of defaulters. Arrears increased from £4,300 in 1884 to £7,180 in 1887, almost £3,000.[36]

Two further land acts were passed, in 1887 and 1891, but although there was no large-scale selling by the landlords their general condition was increasingly deteriorating. They had lost the opportunity to align themselves with the nationalist cause, and political power, both at national and local level, was no longer in their hands. They lacked a sense of identity; they were 'English to the Irish, and Irish to the English'. As the historian, F S L Lyons expressed it: 'Their tragedy was that, hesitating as they did between two worlds, they could never be fully accepted by either ... Caught between unsympathetic governments and resentful tenants they provided a convenient scapegoat for most of the ills of nineteenth-century Ireland.'[37] Now, with their income under attack, it was only a question of time before their demise.

Eventually the Wyndham Land Act of 1903, which gave very favourable terms to the landlords, was passed, and the big sell-out to the tenants began.[38] Under its terms, the entire purchase money was paid in cash to the landlords and a 12 per cent bonus was added to those who made a deal within five years. Now throughout the country there was a huge move to sell as both landlords and tenants realised that the terms of the act could never be bettered. It was sufficient to entice even the larger landlords to rid themselves of their Irish estates. Many, however, retained land for their own use and, as already established, could sell their entire estate to the Land Commission and repurchase the demesne land. In this way several continued to reside as large farmers on their former estates.

The dawn of the twentieth century brought little joy to the Blessington estate. In addition to the problem of mounting arrears, the tenants continued to apply to the Land Commission for rent reviews, thus significantly reducing the income from the estate. In 1881, the annual rental was £6,836; at the beginning of the twentieth century it was £5,574. The question now was not whether, but when, the Downshires would sell. And so the once great dynasties of the Boyle and Hill families, which had dominated the lives of the people of Blessington for over two centuries, quietly came to an end as the tenants bought out their holdings. They had come, according to the Hill motto, 'By God and the Sword', but left without as much as a whimper.

95 The Market House and the Downshire monument

The Land Commission finally completed the sale in 1908. The total purchase money was £106,622, or twenty times the annual rental. The withdrawal of the Downshires from their Irish estates was not a sudden cut-off; for several years they visited Blessington to hold shooting parties at the lodge they had built at Ballylow. But following the War of Independence, when the lodge was burnt, the visits ceased. The association with the north of Ireland lasted a little longer, although the sixth marquis, under whose stewardship the sale to the tenants took place, preferred to stay at the relatively modest Murlough House at Dundrum in county Down rather than at Hillsborough Castle. Eventually the upkeep of the castle proved too much for the resources of the estate and it was let in the early part of the twentieth century to Sir Thomas Dixon. In 1922, it was purchased by the Ministry of Works in London, and used as the residence of the Governor of Northern Ireland until that office was abolished in 1972.[39] The castle underwent major refurbishment in the 1980s and is now used as the official residence of the Secretary of State for Northern Ireland.

Today, the principal reminders of the Boyle and Hill families in Blessington are the church of St Mary's, the agent's house (now the Downshire Hotel), the Market House (now the Credit Union House), the inn (now the Ulster Bank) and the monument in the square commemorating the coming of age in 1865 of the Earl of Hillsborough, later the fifth Marquis of Downshire.

ॐ Epilogue

Until this century the Blessington demesne, the heart of the estate, had remained virtually intact since the time of Archbishop Boyle; it survived the destruction of his mansion and continued to be farmed as one unit until very recently. Some of the features of Boyle's gardens give a hint of the grandeur that was once part of this landscape – the fortification that separated the formal gardens from what were known as the "bastion fields", the ornamental ponds and the avenue linking the big house to St Mary's Church. Now all is changing and a major new town centre with shopping, leisure and residential facilities is altering Blessington's former rural character. But the new development is also opening up the demesne land to the public and so for the first time the people of Blessington will be free to walk in the once grand pleasure gardens of the Boyles and the Downshires.

Today the challenge facing Blessington is to develop into a genuine community, open and inclusive, which will embrace old and young, native born as well as new arrivals, all inspired with a vision for the future and a feeling of connectedness with those who share their neighbourhood. This will lead to a sense of cohesion and pride in a common identity; in other words, a sense of place.

For the inhabitants of Blessington, this sense of place can be enhanced by an appreciation of its past history and a realisation that the bitterness of past divisions has long gone. The landed estate system which for almost two hundred and fifty years shaped the Blessington area was based on a class and a religious divide that left its own legacy of suspicion and resentment – what the historian, FSL Lyons, called 'an anarchy in the mind and in the heart, an anarchy which forbade not just unity of territories, but also "unity of being", an anarchy that sprang from the collision within a small and intimate island of seemingly irreconcilable cultures, unable to live together or live apart, caught inextricably in the web of their tragic history'.[1]

Where is Blessington's inspiration for the future to come from? The diarist Elizabeth Smith provides a lead. In 1845, when she felt that the local priest in Valleymount, Father Germaine, was undermining the school under her patronage at Baltiboys, she protested to the Catholic Archbishop of Dublin. The archbishop sent for Father Germaine who 'returned much changed', and according to Mrs Smith 'we are to walk through the parish hereafter hand in hand doing good and peace ensuing'. As the people of Blessington walk 'the great avenue' which once connected St. Mary's Church to Boyle's mansion and which will now link the old town to its new centre, they can be mindful of Elizabeth Smith's remark. It could serve as a motto for the future community of Blessington – 'walking hand in hand, doing good and peace ensuing'.

[1] Lyons 1982: 177.

ꙮ Appendix

List of Tenants on the Blessington Estate, 1850.

Tenants and Townlands[a]	Holdings[b]	Annual Rent		
Ballydonnell				
Carney, Anthony (held in common)	695	£4	12s	4d
Carney, Edward		£14	15s	4d
Carney, Maurice		£8	15s	4d
Carney, Peter		£8	15s	4d
Commons, Thomas	320	£13	0s	0d
Flood, Francis	580	£17	10s	10d
Ballylow				
Brady, John	7	£9	0s	0d
Brady, Widow	7	£8	0s	0d
Carney, Edward	14	£24	10s	0d
Fitzsimons, John	5	£6	4s	0d
Fitzsimons, Robert	14	£23	0s	0d
Lawler, Edward	7	£8	0s	0d
McEvoy, Andrew	5	£3	0s	0d
Moran, Peter	14	£15	14s	0d
Neil, John	7	£9	4s	0d
Purcell, Widow	5	£4	4s	0d
Sheridan, Bryan	14	£19	4s	0d
Ballynabrocky				
Bourke, Patrick	306	£8	8s	0d
Hawkins, Richard	674	£20	0s	0d
Lynch, Peter	465	£18	17s	10d
Lynch, William	344	£18	14s	10d
Purcell, Patrick	278	£8	8s	4d
White, John	674	£22	13s	6d
Ballynasculloge				
Dowling, Anthony	403	£61	7s	0d
Dowling, Widow	403	£61	7s	0d
Healy, Michael	244	£61	4s	0d
Healy, Richard	123	£50	15s	8d
Ballynatona				
Flood, Widow	47	£5	2s	0d

Tenants and Townlands	Holdings	Annual Rent		
Flood, William	89	£10	3s	8d
Higgins, James	136	£16	13s	6d
Higgins, Michael	68	£6	14s	0d
Higgins, Nicholas	68	£6	14s	0d
Murphy, Austin	93	£8	14s	2d
Murphy, James	89	£7	8s	0d
Murphy, John	89	£8	14s	2d
Ballysmuttan Lower				
Byrne, Widow	56	£13	18s	6d
Murphy, James	71	£14	18s	2d
Murphy, Widow	106	£13	16s	8d
Walsh, John	53	£11	1s	2d
Walsh, William	53	£9	1s	0d
Ballysmuttan Upper				
Mullally, John (held in common)	194	£23	15s	0d
Mullally, Patrick		£23	15s	0d
Ballyward				
Finnemore, John	339	£144	0s	0d
Blackhall (county Kildare)				
Beaghan, George	60	£41	12s	6d
Beaghan, James	50	£41	11s	6d
Byrne, Widow E	19	£17	5s	0d
Currin, Widow	82	£80	0s	0d
Miley, Widow	58	£40	1s	8d
Mullee, Denis	37	£24	0s	0d
Walsh, James	21	£17	6s	2d
Blackrock				
Clarke, Patrick	44	£14	6s	6d
Dall, James and G	87	£23	4s	0d
Duffy, James	25	£6	12s	6d
Hanlon, Luke	44	£14	6s	6d
Hanlon, Philip	10	£2	18s	0d
Blessington, (town)[c]				
Boothman, Thomas	1	£3	4s	2d
Boothman, Thomas	–	£3	11s	0d
Boothman, Thomas	–	£3	0s	10d
Bourke, Roger	1	£14	15s	0d
Conway, John	–	£6	0s	0d
Dallon, James	–	£1	11s	8d
Darker, reps of G[d]	3	£11	3s	6d
Deceise, William	–	£6	0s	0d

Tenants and Townlands	Holdings	Annual Rent		
Deevy, James	1	£3	1s	0d
Doran, James junior	6	£3	10s	0d
Doran, James senior	–	£3	0s	10d
Doran, reps of Joseph	–	£3	0s	10d
Dowling, John	–	£2	16s	6d
Dowling, reps of John	2	£1	0s	6d
Dowling, reps of John	–	£6	0s	0d
Eager, reps of Henry	3	£6	17s	0d
Eager, Joseph B	–	£7	8s	10d
Ebbs, Messrs	4	£20	4s	0d
Finnemore, Widow	–	£3	6s	0d
Freeman, Simon	–	£7	8s	0d
Gyves, reps of Richard	–	£4	13s	2d
Hall, Mary	–	£5	11s	4d
Handbidge, John	4	£5	5s	0d
Handbidge, John	–	£4	12s	10d
Ivers, James	–	£3	0s	0d
Kearns, Michael	–	£2	10s	0d
Kelly, Edward	–	£4	13s	0d
Lee, William	–	£4	13s	0d
Martin, Thomas	–	£3	0s	6d
Merrey, William	3	£1	4s	0d
Merrey, William	–	£3	10s	2d
Merrey, William G	1	£2	0s	0d
Mooney, Joseph	1	£12	0s	0d
Mulloy, Martin	–	£4	12s	10d
Murray, reps of George	–	£2	16s	4d
Murray, reps of George	–	£1	8s	8d
Owen, William	41	£33	4s	8d
Oxford, George	–	£3	14s	4d
Oxford, reps of James	–	£3	14s	2d
Oxford, reps of James	–	£3	0s	10d
Payne, Jonathan	–	£12	0s	0d
Power, Michael	–	£1	10s	0d
Robinson, Doctor	–	£20	0s	4d
Rueben, reps of Paul	–	£4	12s	10d
Sergeant, James	–	£4	12s	10d
Sergeant, Nicholas	–	£1	11s	6d
St Laurence, reps of	1	£2	10s	6d
St Laurence, reps of	–	£5	11s	0d
Trousdall, reps of	1	£3	3s	4d

Tenants and Townlands	Holdings	Annual Rent		
Tyrrell, Eugene	–	£11	1s	10d
Wallace, Henry	–	£7	8s	0d
Wallace, Thomas	–	£7	8s	0d
Whittle, Andrew	–	£4	12s	10d
Wickham, reps of		£7	1s	0d
Blessington, Deerpark				
Owen, William	300	n/g		
Blessington, Demesnec				
Carpenter, Michael	5	£9	0s	0d
Conway, John	6	£2	0s	0d
Craddock, James	1	£9	0s	0d
Dallon, James	5	£8	5s	0d
Deceise, William	9	£10	0s	0d
Doran, James junior	6	£12	0s	0d
Doyle, James	6	£6	12s	4d
Doyle, James	13	£14	1s	4d
Doyle, James	–	£2	11s	4d
Freeman, Richard	6	£13	0s	0d
Gyves, John	4	£8	10s	6d
Gyves, John	4	£2	10s	0d
Hall, Mary	7	£6	13s	2d
Kavanagh, John	2	£2	7s	2d
Kavanagh, John	8	£7	15s	8d
Kilbee, Charles	5	£4	15s	4d
Merrey, William	–	£3	0s	10d
Owen, William	45	n/g		
Owen, William	194	n/g		
Sargeant, Nicholas	2	£1	13s	4d
Wallace, Henry	2	£2	1s	2d
Wallace, Henry	2	£3	6s	0d
Blessington, Merrylands				
Merrey, William G	8	£5	6s	0d
Butterhill				
Boothman, John	67	£68	5s	4d
Browne, Mathew	117	£120	0s	0d
Byrne, Dennis	15	£15	18s	0d
Deevey, William	53	£40	1s	0d
Deevy, Widow	32	£21	10s	0d
Hall, Mary	34	£22	0s	10d
Hanlon, reps of P	25	£15	6s	0d
Hanlon, Philip	14	£9	3s	4d

Tenants and Townlands	Holdings	Annual Rent		
Keegan, Patrick	25	£17	6s	0d
McDaniel, Charles	12	£10	18s	8d
Short, Patrick	11	£7	2s	2d
Smith, Robert	80	£55	6s	6d
Crosscoolharbour (*county Kildare)				
Archer, Rev JF	6	£8	14s	0d
Archer, Rev JF★	18	£15	11s	8d
Boothman, Thomas	59	£69	10s	0d
Boothman, Thomas	143	£175	7s	0d
Breen, Timothy	3	£4	5s	6d
Breen, Timothy	10	£16	0s	0d
Broe, Widow★		£2	1s	6d
Brown, John	117	£118	14s	4d
Brown, Michael	169	£173	8s	10d
Clarke, Stephen★	19	£15	10s	4d
Fearis, Peter	84	£74	2s	0d
Fearis, Peter junior	64	£52	8s	10d
Fearis, Widow	44	£38	12s	6d
Kelly, Patrick★	19	£16	15s	4d
Kelly, William★	19	£16	6s	4d
Lynch, John★	10	£7	17s	10d
Panton, Widow	47	£58	15s	4d
Panton, Widow	74	£70	8s	8d
Roache, Thomas★	6	£5	11s	4d
Walsh, Christopher★	21	£16	2s	0d
Dillonsdown				
Connolly, Christopher	18	£10	4s	6d
Dowdal, Laurence	16	£9	10s	0d
Doyle, Widow	3	£2	1s	0d
Flanigan, Bryan	13	£6	0s	0d
Kelly, William	18	£10	14s	4d
Lawler, Widow	5	£2	3s	4d
Panton, Widow	65	£28	13s	6d
Roache, Patrick	6	£3	0s	10d
Edmondstown				
Boothman, William	2	£2	5s	0d
Panton, Widow	23	£19	9s	0d
Haylands				
Bermingham, William	–	£8	0s	0d
Bourke, Roger	5	£3	6s	4d
Bourke, Roger	6	£5	14s	2d

Tenants and Townlands	Holdings	Annual Rent		
Clarke, Thomas	6	£4	19s	6d
Dolan and Devine	–	£7	10s	0s
Doran, reps of Joseph	4	£3	6s	0d
Doran, reps of Joseph	2	£1	7s	4d
Doran, reps of Joseph	6	£5	6s	2d
Doran, reps of Joseph	7	£5	19s	10d
Doran, reps of Joseph	7	£4	11s	4d
Doran, reps of Joseph	9	£8	8s	2d
Doran, reps of Joseph	13	£11	19s	2d
Mooney and Mulligan	11	£5	14s	4d
Mooney, Benjamin	8	£10	0s	0d
Mulligan, Robert	29	£32	0s	0d
Murphy and Byrne	–	£7	10s	0d
Sergeant, Nicholas	5	£2	9s	6d
Sergeant, Nicholas	7	£3	11s	8d
Sergeant, Nicholas	8	£5	6s	10d
Trousdall, reps of	4	£3	0s	8d
Hempstown				
Boothman, William	60	£70	6s	0d
Brownrigg, reps of William	126	£147	4s	0d
Cullen, Thomas	53	£67	6s	0d
Lamb, Michael	19	£24	10s	0d
Olligan, Patrick	19	£24	10s	0d
Holyvalley				
Walshe, reps of Robert	58	£39	13s	8d
Knockieran Lower				
Carroll, Patrick	2	£2	17s	4d
Delany, Michael	3	£2	17s	2d
Dowling John	14	£13	2s	10d
Hall, Robert	112	£91	0s	0d
Hanlon, B and J Jones	3	£2	11s	2d
Hanlon, Bryan	16	£12	5s	4d
Jones, James	9	£5	19s	0d
Keogh, Edward	2	£2	3s	0d
Keogh, Martin	53	£40	11s	0d
McDaniel, Widow	32	£19	1s	2d
Merrey, William	3	£2	17s	4d
Moore, Patrick	2	£2	17s	4d
Reilly, Charles	4	£2	17s	4d
Reilly, Charles	14	£6	12s	0d
Reilly, Charles	16	£12	6s	0d

Tenants and Townlands	Holdings	Annual Rent		
Sargeant, Nicholas	3	£2	17s	4d
Scully, Edward	5	£4	3s	6d
Knockieran Upper				
Clarke, Thomas	20	£8	10s	4d
Clarke, William	38	£19	2s	0d
Farrell, Widow	1		10s	0d
Hanlon, James	5	£2	0s	od
Hanlon, James	11	£4	18s	0d
Hanlon, James	46	£23	18s	4d
Nowlan, Andrew	32	£12	6s	4d
Scully, Edward	3	£1	6s	4d
Lugnagun				
Deevey, James	87	£10	14s	0d
Deevey, John	58	£10	8s	10d
Hastings, Miles	33	£5	0s	0d
Hastings, Widow	33	£5	0s	0d
Lyons, Daniel	15	£2	5s	8d
Mahon, Widow	14	£2	5s	8d
Phibbs, Laurence	42	£9	4s	4d
Phibbs, Patrick	42	£9	4s	4d
Rickardson and Lyons	28	£4	14s	4d
Rickardson, Lawrence	66	£11	15s	8d
Newtown Park (county Kildare)				
Bourke, John	12	£10	12s	2d
Broe, James	36	£32	7s	6d
Byrne, Richard	9	£5	0s	0d
Cullen, John	107	£50	0s	0d
Dallen, James	6	£5	14s	10d
Doyle, James	3	£4	2s	0d
Doyle, James	4	£4	2s	0d
Hanning, James	7	£11	5s	0d
Jones, Michael	11	£4	13s	8d
Kavanagh, John	6	£5	16s	0d
Kavanagh, John	6	£5	1s	4d
Kavanagh, John	7	£6	0s	4d
Lawless, Widow	11	£4	13s	4d
Lyons, Patrick	18	£16	7s	8d
Mulally, Widow	4	£2	2s	0d
Ryan, John	6	£3	11s	8d
Ryan, John	8	£7	0s	6d
Ryan, John	8	£7	0s	4d

Tenants and Townlands	Holdings	Annual Rent		
Newtown Great (county Kildare)				
Byrne, John	59	£47	17s	0d
Byrne, Peter	59	£48	0s	6d
Byrne, Laurence	30	£23	15s	0d
Mullee, Peter	160	£110	0s	0d
Walsh, James	125	£100	15s	2d
Byrne, Widow	30	£23	15s	0d
Newtown Little (county Kildare)				
Boothman, Thomas	6	£8	4s	4d
Hall, Mary	15	£14	10s	0d
White, Michael	1	£1	0s	0d
Oldcourte				
Allen, John	–	£1	10s	0d
Brennan, Murtagh	–	£2	15s	4d
Brown, Mathew	–	£3	0s	0d
Finnemore, John	11	£10	10s	0d
Fox, John	–	£3	0s	0d
Hanlon, Thomas	–	£27	0s	0d
Healy, Carbery	–	£50	0s	0d
Keogh, Hugh	–	£7	4s	6d
Keogh, Widow	–	£2	15s	4d
Lawler, Widow and John	245	£96	19s	2d
Lawler, William	–	£9	0s	0d
Mergin, John	–	£7	10s	0d
Mooney, James	14	£10	0s	0d
Murphy, P and P Olligan	49	£30	0s	0d
Murphy, Widow	–	£5	19s	0d
Murphy, Widow	–	£1	0s	0d
Olligan, Patrick	81	£60	0s	0d
Patrickson, reps of John	249	£96	1s	0d
Smith, John	–	£7	0s	0d
White, Thomas	–	£64	0s	0d
Paddocks				
Boothman, William	42	£24	1s	6d
Boothman, William	48	£42	15s	6d
Doran, James senior	10	£22	0s	8d
Wickam, reps	35	£45	2s	10d
Santryhill				
Panton, Widow	3	£3	15s	6d
Panton, Widow	17	£11	14s	6d

Tenants and Townlands	Holdings	Annual Rent		
Segrave's Castle (county Kildare)				
Clarke, reps of T	30	£40	11s	8d
Threecastles				
Begley, John	49	£40	0s	0d
Cooke, Widow	5	£7	8s	8d
Cooke, Widow	10	£9	1s	8d
Farley, Michael	19	£8	11s	8d
Kilbee, Charles	202	£120	0s	0d
Panton, Widow	59	£72	16s	8d
Tallon, Garret	65	£37	16s	10d
Tallon, Joseph	13	£5	14s	2d
Tallon, Joseph	49	£28	7s	8d
White, Thomas	5	£6	2s	0d
Wilson, reps of A	49	£42	18s	0d
Wilson, Thomas	145	£154	3s	2d
Walshestown (county Kildare)				
James Walsh	21	£20	0s	0d
James Walsh	25	£20	0s	0d
James Walsh	58	£48	10s	0d

Source: PRONI D.671/R2/79 and 80.

a   Unlike Griffith's Valuation the Rentals only list tenants holding directly from the Downshires. Rathnabo is incorporated into Blackrock and Butterhill.

b   The size of holdings is given to the nearest acre. All are in county Wicklow unless county Kildare is specified. Several entries for the same tenants means they had more than one holding.

c   In Blessington Town and Blessington Demesne only holdings above half an acre are given; most were less than a quarter.

d   'Reps' indicates that the original tenant was no longer in possession through death or some other cause and a new tenant, generally a family member, had taken over the holding.

e   The acreage of some holdings in Oldcourt is not given; these belonged to undertenants of John Patrickson and Charles Lilly who had been granted the land by the first Marquis of Downshire in 1791. The Downshire administration was at the time taking legal action to regain possession of the land.

ॐ Acknowledgements

Many hours were spent in research institutions and I wish to acknowledge the help I received from the Keeper of the Records, the staff and especially Ian Montgomery of the Public Records Office of Northern Ireland; the directors and staff of the National Library and the National Archives in Dublin; and the librarians in the Representative Church Body, the Dublin Diocesan Archives, and the Irish Architectural Archives. I am particularly indebted to Caroline de Robeck, her late husband, Martin, and her son, John, for permission to examine and use the estate papers in the family home at Gowran Grange, near Naas.

Many other people helped in a variety of ways, for which I am grateful: Michael Dempsey for sharing his knowledge of the Blessington estate and allowing me the use of the material he had collected over the years; members of the Blessington Local and Family History Society and especially Janet Halligan for their support; Jim Corley for making available material in his possession; Vincent Byrne for a copy of the painting of the mill; Rupert Macauley for his help in regard to Ballyward House; members of the vestry committee for permission to photograph memorials in St Mary's Church; Eamonn Fitzsimons who pointed me in the right direction with regard to the Leeson family; Very Rev Father Kevin Lyons, PP, Crosschapel, and Margaret Flynn in Blessington Library.

I also wish to thank the many people and organisations who helped with illustrative material for the book: Mrs Patricia Pelly, Dermot James and Seamus Ó Maithiú for the portraits of the Smiths; Mrs J Leighton of the Diocese of Armagh for her assistance in obtaining a copy of the portrait of Archbishop Boyle; Lisa Courtney of Margaret Gowen, Archaeological Consultants, for a copy of John Longfield's map of Blessington Demesne; members of the Byrne family of Slade Valley who introduced me to the use of digital photography; and the National Photographic Archives. Portraits of the Downshire family and prints illustrating the 1798 Rebellion are by courtesy of the National Gallery of Ireland, the Ulster Museum, the National Portrait Gallery, and the National Army Museum in London. The fourth marquis proved to be most elusive to trace but with the help of the Hillsborough Castle administration (especially John Chiddick, Commander David Maxwell and David Anderson) and Harrison Photography of Belfast we are able to reproduce his portrait.

The knowledge that someone in the publishing world believed in the worth of the undertaking was very important so my thanks to Rena Dardis of Anvil Books, my editor. And I must record my appreciation to the Heritage Council of Ireland for their generous grant towards the book's publication.

Finally, thanks to the members of my own family: to Nicholas who helped with the maps, to Maurice, Mary-Liz, and Barbara, who watched as the journey unfolded, and to Anton who walked the road with me.

✌ Abbreviations

BL	Bodleian Library, Oxford
BM	British Museum
DDA	Dublin Diocesan Archives
GO	Genealogical Office
HMC	Historical Manuscript Commission
IAA	Irish Architectural Archives
IAR	Irish Arts Review
NAI	National Archives, Ireland
NLI	National Library of Ireland
OP	Official Papers
OS	Ordnance Survey
PRONI	Public Record Office of Northern Ireland
RC	Record Commission
RCB	Representative Church Body
RLFC	Relief Commission
RSAIJ	Royal Society of Antiquaries of Ireland Journal
SOC	State of the Country Papers
UAHS	Ulster Architectural Heritage Society
UHF	Ulster Historical Foundation
UM	Ulster Museum
UJA	Ulster Journal of Archaeology

Notes and Sources

1 The Struggle for Land

1 There are other signs of Christian settlements in the area. A church traditionally associated with St Brigid of Kildare was situated at Shankill (the name means old church) close to the Neolithic passage grave on Seefinn mountain, thirteen kilometres from Blessington. The church in turn was connected by a mountain track to a Christian settlement at Kilmosanctan in Glenasmole. Another old pilgrim road passed through the neighbourhood of Blessington, connecting the monastic settlement of Kilnamanagh in Tallaght with St Kevin's monastery in Glendalough.

2 The motte was a pudding-shaped earthen mound with a flat top, surrounded by a ditch, which was built by the Normans as a base for a wooden tower. The bailey was a fortified rectangular enclosure, also surrounded by a ditch and joined to the motte by a wooden bridge. By the beginning of the thirteenth century, this primitive type of fortification was being replaced by stone castles.

3 This resulted in a new landowning class, the 'adventurers', who supplied money for the army and in return were given land, either to live on or to sell.

2 The Boyle Dynasty

1 Stephen & Lee 1917: 1021-4.

2 Canny 1982: 19-21.

3 ibid: 19.

4 ibid: 46-51.

5 ibid: 30-1 and 44-5.

6 Most sources give his date of birth as approximately 1609. However, in a letter written by Boyle in 1679 to his cousin, Lady Ranelagh, a daughter of the Earl of Cork, he states that he was then about sixty-four years of age, which would put his date of birth at 1615.

7 NLI GO MS 161.

8 HMC vol 1, 1905: 611.

9 PRONI D.665/1 and 2; Stokes 1893: 342-6.

10 PRONI D.671/D2/2/1.

11 The first citizen of the town.

12 IAA, 89/18, agreements between Boyle and Lucas and Boyle and

Browne, and Blessington House building accounts. *See also* de Breffny 1989: 73-7.

13 HMC Report 11, Appendix.7, 1888: 12. When Boyle was elevated to the See of Armagh in 1678 his income was augmented by the rents from the large estates held by the diocese. *See* NLI de Vesci MSS, rent roll of the estate of the Archbishop of Armagh, microfilm, positive 6797.

14 TCD MSS 1, 13:86. Quoted by de Breffny 1989:73. Molyneux was a member of an English family that had come from Calais to Ireland in the 1570s. He was a diplomat and MP for Trinity College.

15 Craig 1989: 146.

16 Statute acres are used generally in the text: an Irish acre equals 1.62 statute acres.

17 Reilly 2000.

18 Mooney 1989: 27. Archdeacon Bulkeley also owned an estate in Dunlavin, and both estates eventually became the property of the Tynte family of Cork, following the marriage of Hester Bulkeley, one of the archdeacon's descendants, to James Worth Tynte in 1702.

19 RCB Blessington Parish Register, P.651 1.1.

20 The altar vessels, in use until 1895, were stolen from the Glebe House. They were recovered badly damaged some time later and only two were repairable.

21 Jigginstown refers to Thomas Wentworth's mansion near Naas begun in the 1630s but never completed.

22 RCB Blessington Parish Register, P.651 1.1.

23 HMC, Report 6, Appendix, 1877: 743.

24 BM Add. MS 34,772, folio 1-4.

25 The word 'tories' comes from the Irish *toraidhe* meaning raider.

26 HMC, Report 6, Appendix, 1877: 735.

27 Lydon 1998: 209.

28 The term 'rapparee' is interchangeable with 'tory' and the rapparees in question were most likely the Wicklow O'Byrnes and O'Tooles.

29 Sadlier 1928: 129.

30 BL, MS Rawl.C.984, folio 85.

31 ibid, folio 86.

32 PRONI D.671/D2/1

33 NLI, G.O. MS. 161; PRONI D.671/02/1/1; Stokes 1893 and Nichols 1745.

34 Stokes 1893: 343.

35 Gibbs 1912: 190-1.

36 Stephen & Lee 1917: 1021.

37 www.iol.ie/cbcmonks/history.

38 RCB Blessington Parish Register, P. 651 1 1.

39 Inter-relationships were common within families of the upper classes in Ireland. The Cootes were also intermarried with the Hills of Hillsborough, Rose Coote's mother being Penelope Hill, daughter of Arthur Hill.
40 Longworth Dames 1893: 430-1.
41 *See:* 'Notes on Illustrations', frontispiece.
42 Charles John Gardiner later inherited the Stewart estates and although he had no direct connection with the estate in Blessington, added Earl of Blessington to his titles in 1816. His wife, Margaret or Marguerite Power, became a well known socialite.
43 PRONI D.665/25. *See also* Sadlier 1928: 130.
44 Robert Boyle (1627–91), son of the Earl of Cork, was a leading scientist of his day and gave his name to a scientific principle known as Boyle's Law (the proportional relationship between elasticity and pressure). He was a deeply religious man and financed the translation of the Old and New Testament into Irish. His religious convictions were not at odds with his scientific work, as he believed the empirical study of the world about him provided independent evidence for the work of a creator.

3 The Downshire Connection

1 Hill ended up by marrying Sorley Boy's sister.
2 Maguire 1972: 2-8
3 Stephen & Lee 1917: 879; Maguire 1993: 13.
4 Maguire 1998: 36.
5 PRONI D.671/V/360.
6 PRONI D.607/B/211.
7 PRONI D.671/V/360.
8 Gibbs 1912: 197 and 451.
9 Maguire 1972: 80.
10 PRONI D.607/C/26 and D.607/D/325.
11 PRONI D.607/F/521 and 556.
12 The topography of the estate was dramatically altered in the 1930s when Poulaphouca reservoir was created by flooding the valleys of the Liffey and its tributary, the Kings river.
13 A small portion of Crosscoolharbour townland is also situated in Kildare in the barony of Naas North. In addition, a holding of 30 acres, known as Segrave's Castle, which was detached from the main body of the estate and situated in Naas North, belonged to the Downshires. The five townlands in Kildare (Blackhall, Newtown Park, Newtown Great, Newtown Little and Walshestown) were granted to Morough Boyle in 1703. PRONI D.665/16
14 Griffith's Valuation. *See* 'Notes on Illustrations', no 59.

96 *The Downshire estate in county Down*

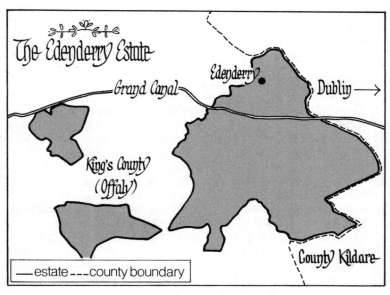

97 *The Downshire estate in Edenderry*

15 Cited in Donnelly 1975: 141-2.
16 Trant 1997: 37-8.

4 The Rebellion of 1798

1 The militia was originally a part-time military force, but was re-established on a full-time basis in 1793 to augment the regular army. Although the officers were mainly Protestant, the rank and file were predominantly Catholic.
2 O'Donnell 1998: 93-106.
3 ibid: 93.
4 PRONI D.607/F/92, 130 and 176.
5 PRONI D.607/F/185.
6 PRONI D.607/F/190.
7 Hill Benson later reported that Mrs Farley's house was also 'rendered a ruin' in the rebellion. PRONI D.671/C/211/3.
8 Myers & McKnight, 1995: 700.
9 DDA Troy Papers, AB2/116/7.
10 PRONI D.607/F/409.
11 NAI M 5513/4.
12 PRONI D.607/G/45. Horseshoe House was at Tinode, five kilometres on the Dublin side of Blessington.
13 ibid.
14 NAI RC 14/10
15 NAI M 5513/4.
16 NAI RC 14/10; OP 61/4/1 and 7; OP 150/4/2.
17 de Quincy quoted by Lydon, 1998: 277.
18 Following her death in 1836, the title Baron Sandys devolved to the second son of the family.
19 PRONI D.607/I/3.
20 Maguire 1972: 91.
21 ibid: 123-4. A 40-shilling freeholder was a person who could vote by virtue of holding a lease for lives on land worth 40s and over per annum after the payment of rent and other charges.
22 Maguire 1993: 14.

5 Bad Debts and Good Neighbours

1 The names combined both his maternal and paternal lineages and were given to the head of the family from then on.
2 PRONI D.671/C/211/4.
3 Maguire 1972: 87.
4 Edward Gibbon Wakefield was an English political activist and writer who professed radical views on the reform of society during the first

half of the nineteenth century. Quoted in Maguire1972: 85.

5   E. Gaskell, *Wives and Daughters,* ch 31, quoted in Maguire 1972: 89.

6   Maguire 1972: 86-7.

7   Tillyard 1995: 211–26.

8   ibid: 258: and 165–7.

9   The de Robeck family were of Swedish origin, as is their title. The second baron, John Henry, fought with the French in America and subsequently found his way to Ireland, where in 1789 he married Anne, the daughter and sole heiress of Richard Fitzpatrick, the second son of Lord Gowran. It was through this alliance that the de Robecks inherited their Irish estates. They are the only landed family who retain some of their original estate and still live in the area.

10 Trant 1997: 37-41.

11 NAI M 5690.

12 Quoted in Butler & O'Kelly 2000: 14.

13 PRONI D.665/14; NAI M 5690

14 Pelly & Tod 1991: vii.

15 Thomson & McGusty 1980: xii-xiii.

16 Pelly & Tod 1991: 9.

17 ibid: 53 and 479.

18 ibid: 524 and 78.

6 Land Tenure and Agents

1   Donnelly 1975: 14.

2   Trant 1997: 78-80.

3   PRONI D.671/C/230/34.

4   PRONI D.671/C/228/6.

5   Trant 1997: 56-66.

6   Lease document in private hands.

7   For an explanation of the term 40-shilling freeholders see note 21 for Chapter 4. In 1829 with the passing of Catholic Emancipation, the franchise was raised to £10 leaseholders and over.

8   Trant 1997: 67.

9   Lease document in private hands.

10 In 1809, no action was recorded when the agent, Hill Benson, pointed out that the leaseholders in Oldcourt, William and John Patrickson and Charles Lilly, had not fulfilled their covenants with regard to building and planting. Thirty-five years later, John Murray's brother, Thomas, when giving evidence to the Devon Commission said that many of the covenants were never enforced and several clauses, such as the obligation to use a specific mill, were long outdated.

11 PRONI D.671/A5/3/8.

12 Maguire 1972: 91-2.
13 Maguire 1972:125-9. The scheme later attracted the attention of Wakefield as an example of extortion of the helpless tenantry. Such schemes, he declared, were 'fraught with injustice', and in the long run 'pregnant with mischief to the country' as well as detrimental to the landlord class. Downpatrick was a 'potwalloper borough', which meant that £5 householders had a vote prior to 1832. Potwallopers were defined as householders who controlled access to their own front door and cooking facilities.
14 Maguire 1972: 93-4.
15 ibid: 155-65 and 67.
16 Grand Juries were a form of local government and were made up of a high sheriff and a jury of between 12 and 23 men selected from among the leading men of property in the county. Initially their function was to decide if specific indictments should proceed to trial, but by the nineteenth century their role was expanded to include the power to levy a local tax to pay for the upkeep of roads and bridges, the building and repair of jails and courthouses, and the establishment of infirmaries, lunatic asylums and fever hospitals in the county. The Grand Juries were mainly seen as the preserve of the landlords, and were replaced by the Local Government Act of 1898.
17 Trant 1997: 27-8.
18 PRONI D.671/C/211/1-12.
19 Maguire 1972: 188.
20 Pelly & Tod 1991: 67.
21 PRONI D.671/C/214/121.
22 PRONI D.671/C/214/366.
23 PRONI D.671/A5/3/22.
24 Flower 1978: 37
25 PRONI D.671/C/214/401 and 380.
26 Pelly & Tod 1991: 55.
27 PRONI D.671/C/213/7; 230/58.
28 Pelly & Tod 1991: 161, 56 and 162.
29 PRONI D.671/213/8 and 9.
30 Pelly & Tod 1991: 485.

7 The Tenants

1 Donnelly 1975: 16-20.
2 By the 1830s the quarrying in Kilbride had mainly ceased and the quarry owner, Patrick Olligan, had transferred his business to Ballyknockan. According to local tradition, the quarry workers from Kilbride moved with him, and one account records that 'every Monday morning before daybreak about four hundred stone-cutters

set out from Kilbride and walked the ten-mile journey to Ballyknockan, arriving before six o'clock to begin the day's work. During the week they lodged with the local people and left for their homes on Saturday afternoon'. Brady 1963: 180.

3 PRONI D.671/C/214/358. The Kilwarlin estate, part of the Downshire lands in the north, was centred on Hillsborough.

4 PRONI D.671/C/230/135; C/214/203 and 318.

5 PRONI D.671/C/230/6.

6 PRONI D.671/C/211/3; R2/7, 8, 46 and 117; C/230/27.

7 PRONI D.671/R2/54; C/228/6 and A33/1.

8 PRONI D.671/C/230/31.

9 Pelly & Tod 1991: x.

10 Hill 1846: 16-7.

11 NLI OS Names Book for Wicklow. The Ordnance Survey was a detailed mapping of the country undertaken between 1825 and 1841 as a prelude to the valuation of rateable property.

12 PRONI D.671/C/230/34 and 215/32.

13 Trant 1997: 51-4 and 138-9.

14 Pelly & Tod 1991: x and 286-96.

15 NLI OS Names Book for Wicklow.

8 Rent and Arrears

John Foster was the last Speaker of the Irish House of Commons

1 PRONI D.671/C/211/3; C/228/9.

2 PRONI D.671/C/214/71.

3 Maguire 1972: 29-37. The British and Irish exchequers were amalgamated in 1826; the Irish pound was then equal to 18s 5d British currency.

4 PRONI D.671/R2/19 and 24.

5 PRONI D.671/C/214/34 and 52.

6 PRONI D.671/C/214/168.

7 PRONI D.671/A5/3; R2/46.

8 In the early 1830s the marquis successfully got a reversal of an original lease granted in perpetuity in 1679 to Isaac Eccles.

9 Trant 1997: 104-5.

10 PRONI D.671/C/214/330 and 337.

11 PRONI D.671/C/218/1-4.

12 PRONI D.671/C/214/337; C/218/4.

13 PRONI D.671//C214/340 and 342.

14 NAI SOC 2374/34.

15 PRONI D.671/R2/55.

16 Malcomson 1978: 312.

17 PRONI D.671/C/214/378 and 377.
18 Pelly & Tod 1991: 295.
19 Thomson & McGusty 1980: xviii.
20 Quoted in Maguire 1972: 146.
21 PRONI D.671/C/214/120
22 PRONI D.671/C/211/4.
23 PRONI D.671/C/214/95, 99 and 116. He was later to make a bid, albeit unsuccessfully, for another holding on the estate.
24 PRONI D.671/C/214/99.
25 PRONI D.671/C/214/214, 254 and 276. One member of the Cullen family retained a holding in Hempstown.
26 PRONI D.671/C/215/7 and 15.
27 Pelly & Tod 1991: 182.
28 PRONI D.671/C/215/30.

9 The Landlord's Role

Thomas Drummond was Under Secretary for Ireland from 1835 to 1840

 1 PRONI D.671/C/211/3.
 2 PRONI D.671/C/228/1-4.
 3 PRONI D.671/C/211/3.
 4 RCB, Blessington Parish Register; PRONI D.671/C/211/3.
 5 PRONI D.671/C/227/1-7
 6 The town did not have a Catholic church until 1946, when the original schoolhouse was consecrated as a place of worship.
 7 PRONI D.671/C/211/3.
 8 PRONI D.671/C/228/8.
 9 PRONI D.671/C/217/1-7.
10 PRONI D.671/C/214/259.
11 PRONI D.671/C/220/3-13. The present Annalecky Inn between Blessington and Baltinglass was one of the tollhouses on the road.
12 PRONI D.671/A5/3/57; C/214/75.
13 PRONI D.671/C/214/67 and 81.
14 PRONI D.671/C/214/89B and 90.
15 PRONI D.671/C/214/121; C/226/7.
16 PRONI D.671/R2/46; C/214/164.
17 PRONI D.671/R2/10; A5/3/3; C/230/9.
18 PRONI D.671/C/230/1; C/214/86.
19 PRONI D.671/C/214/109, 112 and 114.
20 PRONI D.671/C/214/35 and 287.
21 Trant 1997: 30-1.
22 PRONI D.671/C/214/122.
23 PRONI D.671/C/214/125; C/230/21.
24 PRONI D.671/C/214/304; 333; 335; 337, 301 and 300.
25 PRONI D.671/C/215/19 and 14.

26 PRONI D.671/C/214/341; C/230/42.
27 PRONI D.671/C/214/171, 256 and 333.
28 PRONI D.671/C/214/15, 17, 97 and 96.
29 Vaughan 1994: 119.
30 Ó Tuathaigh 1984: 99.
31 Pelly & Tod 1991: 47.
32 ibid: 193-8 and 468.

10 The Famine Years

1 *Belfast Protestant Journal,* 19 April 1845.
2 *Belfast Newsletter,* 25 April 1845.
3 ibid.
4 Hall c.1840: 82.
5 Ó Tuathaigh 1984: 113.
6 Griffith's Valuation – *see* 'Notes on Illustrations', no 59.
7 Guinness & Ryan 1971: 154.
8 Green 2001: 226.
9 The 'Gregory clause' was an amendment to the Poor Law named after its proposer, Sir William Gregory, MP for Dublin city and later married to Augusta Persse who at the end of the century was associated with Yeats and the Irish literary revival.
10 Hannigan 1994: 793.
11 Pelly & Tod 1991: 222 and 228-9.
12 ibid: 261.
13 NAI RLFC3/1/3070; 2/442/8/7238 and 10052.
14 NAI RLFC3/2/442/8/8533.
15 PRONI D.671/V/322.
16 PRONI D.671/V/324.
17 PRONI D.671/R2/72; 74; 78 and 80.
18 PRONI D.671/R2/79 and 84. Local tradition states that thirteen families were evicted, and if this was the case some holdings had been subdivided.
19 Census of Ireland 1841 and 1851.
20 ibid.
21 Blessington was part of Naas Poor Law Union. The building of the workhouse, which was to accommodate 550 people, was commenced in 1839 and its first inmates – five men, one woman and one child – were admitted in August 1841.
22 Kiely c.1995: 33.
23 WS Trench (1880) *Realities of Irish Life.* Cited in O'Connor 1995: 251.
24 NLI MS 4974-5.
25 Pelly & Tod 1991: 312.
26 ibid: 290-1.

11 The Social Round

1 Pelly & Tod 1991: 309.
2 Barry 1982: 23.
3 Pelly & Tod 1991: 517, 438-9 and 416.
4 ibid: 488.
5 ibid: 216 and 348.
6 The bridge was at Ballysmuttan. Pelly & Tod 1991: 417-8.
7 ibid: 455; 457.
8 ibid: 458; 459 and 461.
9 ibid: 462-4.
10 ibid: 467-8.
11 ibid: 467 and 472.
12 ibid: 501.

12 The Final Chapter

1 Foster 1988: 336-7.
2 Donnelly 1975: 135-7.
3 Dooley 2000: 117; Trant 1997: 122-3.
4 PRONI D.671/R2/76,78 and 81.
5 Pelly & Tod 1991: 518-9.
6 PRONI D.671/R2/81.
7 PRONI D.671/V/788.
8 PRONI D.671/R2/100.
9 Maguire 1993: 17-8.
10 Moody 2001: 238.
11 *Kildare Observer* 17 January and 28 February 1880.
12 Lyons 1973: 168.
13 *Kildare Observer* 27 August 1881.
14 ibid 26 February 1880.
15 *Leinster Leader* 11 March 1882.
16 *Kildare Observer* 17 January 1880.
17 PRONI D.671/R2/111; *Kildare Observer,* 28 February and 27 March 1880.
18 *Kildare Observer* 27 August 1881.
19 *Leinster Leader* 21 January 1882; PRONI D.671/R2/111.
20 PRONI D.671/V/788.
21 *Leinster Leader* 21 January 1882.
22 ibid 18 January and 11 February 1882.
23 PRONI D.671/R2/111.
24 PRONI D.671/R2/109 and 110.
25 *Leinster Leader* 8 April 1882. When the Land League was suppressed, the Ladies' Land League, headed by Parnell's sister Anna, was

formed.

26 PRONI D.671/R2/111.

27 *Leinster Leader* 1 April 1882.

28 ibid 21 January 1882.

29 PRONI D.671/R2/108-11.

30 Dooley 2000:121.

31 PRONI D.671/R2/111-3.

32 Edward Gibson, later Lord Ashbourne and Lord Chancellor of Ireland, was responsible for the Purchase of Land (Ireland) Act of 1885, whereby the Government provided five million pounds to enable the tenants to borrow the whole of the purchase price for their holdings.

33 PRONI D.671/A34/21.

34 ibid.

35 Donnelly 1975: 380-1.

36 PRONI D.671/R2/113-6.

37 Lyons 1982: 22.

38 George Wyndham, Chief Secretary for Ireland, introduced the Irish Land Act of 1903 which enabled an entire estate to be sold if three-quarters of the tenants acquiesced. The money was advanced by the Government to be repaid over 68 years.

39 Maguire 1993: 18-9.

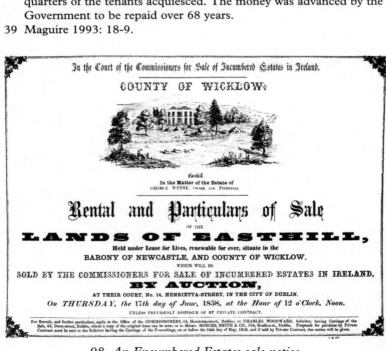

98 *An Encumbered Estates sale notice*

ॐ Notes on Illustrations

The author gratefully acknowledges with thanks all those who supplied prints and photographs and gave permission for reproduction. Every effort has been made to trace the source of copyright material.

Cover: Thomas Roberts, described as 'the most brilliant and short-lived Irish landscape painter of the second half of the eighteenth century', was born in Waterford in 1748 and died in Lisbon in 1778. Among his patrons were the Duke of Leinster and Lord Powerscourt, so he was familiar with the scenery of Wicklow and Kildare. The cover is a detail from his *Ideal Landscape,* probably painted about 1770. (Painting courtesy the National Gallery of Ireland; quote from *The Painters of Ireland c.1660-1920,* Anne Crookshank and the Knight of Glin, Barrie & Jenkins, London 1978)

Back cover: View of Blessington in 1857, from an estate map.

Frontispiece: The painting of Blessington House by Joseph Tudor (1695-1759) only exists in the engraving by John Brooks, dedicated to Viscount Mountjoy, which was published in 1753. (Illustration Terry Myler, based on the copy of the Brooks engraving held by PRONI – ref D 671/P2/4 – courtesy the Keeper of the Records).

1 Before the coming of the Normans, Ireland was developing a native style of architecture based on the Romanesque buildings of Germany and France. RAF Macalister (*The Archaeology of Ireland*) considers Cormac's Chapel at Cashel, built by Cormac MacCarthy, king of Munster, in 1134, the crowning achievement of the Celtic age. (WH Bartlett, *The Scenery and Antiquities of Ireland,* London, vol 1)

2 The seal of Strongbow depicts Norman warriors. (Drawing Terry Myler, based on a nineteenth-century engraving in *The Oxford Illustrated History of Ireland,* ed RF Foster, Oxford 1989)

3 Weston St John Joyce's map in *The Neighbourhood of Dublin* (Gill, Dublin 1939) shows the boundaries of the Pale according to the Statute of 1488. In spite of efforts in 1494 to enclose the whole territory with a double rampart, by 1537 the Pale had shrunk to the area between Dublin and Tallagh. (Drawing Terry Myler)

7 The Fitzgerald family had powerful enemies at the English court, notably Cardinal Wolsey and Anne Boleyn, a member of the rival Butler family. In 1534, the tenth Earl of Kildare and Lord Deputy of

Ireland, Garrett Og, was recalled to London, leaving his son Thomas in charge. Hearing reports that his father had died in the Tower of London, the fiery Thomas rushed to Dublin, confronted the Council of State at St Mary's Abbey in Dublin, threw down the sword of office and declared rebellion against Henry VIII. This dramatic reconstruction includes his Irish piper, O'Keenan. (From a Victorian painting in Dublin Castle)

8 Sir Henry Sidney was Queen Elizabeth's Lord Deputy in 1566 and again from 1575 to 1578. In periods of peace he made tours of the country acccompanied by John Derrick, who made a series of woodcuts depicting the life of the times. The collection was published in 1581 as *The Image of Ireland*. (British Library)

12 Carrickfergus Castle, built between 1180 and 1205 by John de Courcy who came in the wake of the first Cambro-Norman invaders, is probably the most impressive of the Norman castles of Ireland. It was intended for defensive purposes and to impress and intimidate the dispossessed. In the late sixteenth century, when Ulster was still a Gaelic stronghold, the town was the centre of government operations, a northern 'Pale'. By 1700 its importance had declined with the development of Belfast. (WH Bartlett *The Scenery and Antiquities of Ireland*, London, vol l)

13 Edgeworthstown House was the home of a family which came to Ireland in the time of Elizabeth. The house was enlarged and altered by Richard Lovell Edgeworth, father of the writer Maria, who created an open estate which inspired the *Hiberian Magazine* of October 1807 to comment that it was 'unlike those demesnes which are surrounded with lofty walls where the proprietor resides in a kind of secluded grandeur as if more on the defensive from the dreaded irruption of some barbarians than living secure in the midst of countrymen'. (JN Brewer *The Beauties of Ireland*, 1825)

17 The portrait of Archbishop Michael Boyle hangs in Archbishop's House in Armagh. (Courtesy Representative Church Body)

19 The accession to the English throne of William of Orange after the 'glorious' revolution of 1688 sparked an interest in English history in the Netherlands and a number of illustrations of the period were made by Dutch engravers. (*Konincklijcke Beltenis van Karel de II*, Dordrecht 1661. JR Green, *A Short History of the English People*, Macmillan London 1894, vol 3)

20 This map is from a 1787 copy of William Petty's Down Survey. In the aftermath of the confederate war (1641-1653), two surveys – the Civil Survey and the Down Survey, so called because for the first time the information was mapped rather than written down – were undertaken to facilitate the Cromwellian Settlement. The Down

Survey shows the land to be forfeited in all counties with the exception of Clare, Galway, Mayo, Roscommon and Sligo, which had been the focus of the Strafford Inquisition in 1636. It was an enormous undertaking for its day and was noted for the training and organisation of the many surveyors needed to complete the work. Maps at parish level were also produced and were more accurate than anything previously attempted. They show townland boundaries, the owners of the land, acreages and land quality of the forfeited land, and buildings such as castles, churches, houses and mills. (PRONI D.671/D2/1/25)

21 A detail from the Brooks engraving. (PRONI D.671/P2/4)

22 St Mary's Church has been in continuous use as the Church of Ireland parish church since 1683. Originally rectangular in shape, it was altered in the nineteenth century by the addition of side aisles. Its clock is reputed to be the oldest working turret clock in Ireland and the bells, which still ring out, bear the coat of arms of its founder. (The National Library of Ireland).

23 The memorial by William Kidwell is inscribed in Latin. It reads: Michael Boyle STD, Archbishop of Armagh, Primate of all Ireland and highest Bishop of the Kingdom, Chancellor for twenty years and more often Chief Justice of the same. Among his very many services to Church and State at his own expense he founded and built this church of the Blessed Mary of Blessington together with the cemetery (to the Glory of God, for the decent celebration of Divine Worship and the comfort and use of this parish) and provided the Holy Table and Church with flagons, chalices and silver plates and the rest of the furnishings, even adding a handsome belfry with six Tuneful bells. All these things he solemnly dedicated the 24th day of August in the year 1683. In order that there be a perpetual monument of this pious munificence, this memorial stone is inscribed by his son, Morough, Viscount Blessington. "Go and do thou likewise." (Anvil Books)

24 Another of the Dutch engravings. (*Engelants Schouwtoneel verbeeldende het vlugte van Jacobus II*, Amsterdam 1690. JR Green, *A Short History of the English People*, vol 4)

27 Two letters from Archbishop Boyle to his son Morough, then staying at the home of his in-law, the Dowager Lady Mountrath, at Soho Square in London, on 15 and 22 November 1690, give a flavour of conditions in the country in the aftermath of the Battle of the Boyne. Blessington, always vulnerable to attack from Irish rebels who could easily hide out in the hills, was in a state of unrest and Ginkle, who was commanding the army, had sent a small detachment of troops to restore order. Boyle was anxious to ensure that his estate would not suffer any damage and that produce from the demesne could

continue to be sent unimpeded to his house in Dublin. (Bodleian Library, Rawlinson MS, C.984 folio 86, courtesy Michael Dempsey)

30 Monkstown Castle was originally a religious foundation associated with St Mochana. In 1174 Henry II granted it to the Cistercian monks of St Mary's Abbey in Dublin, when it was fortified by a high wall as protection against raids by the O'Byrne and O'Toole Wicklow clans. Following the suppression of the monasteries by Henry VIII in 1539, the lands were given to Sir John Travers, Master of the Ordnance (around this time he also acquired land at Tulfarris near Blessington which later became the property of the Hornidge family). His grand-daughter Mary, wife of James Eustace, Earl of Blessington, inherited his estates. Baltinglass was involved in the Earl of Desmond's rebellion against the crown and the castle was used as a meeting-place by the rebels. Following the failure of the rebellion, Baltinglass fled to Spain where he died. Monkstown and Tulfarris were confiscated by the Crown but were later restored to Mary; they were subsequently inherited by her nephew, Henry Cheevers. The land was again confiscated after the Cromwellian wars but restored to the Cheevers by Charles II in 1660. Shortly after, the castle was acquired by Michael Boyle. His son Morough enlarged and modernised it so that in the early eighteenth century it was considered the second-best residence in south Dublin. When the Boyle line died out in the 1770s, the estate was inherited by the de Vesci and Longford families but by then the castle was said to be in a state of decay. (Engraving after a painting by Gabriel Beranger, the National Library of Ireland)

31 'Illustrations of the Irish Linen Manufactory, County Down', drawn and engraved by W Hincks, was published in London in 1783. Each one was dedicated to a notable county Down person who would have subscribed to the cost. This one, 'Wet and Dry Bleaching – Bleach-Mill', is dedicated to Viscount Kilwarlin, a Hill family title. (Engraving JR Green *A Short History of the English People*, vol IV; caption courtesy the Ulster Museum)

34 Most of the Blessington estate lay within the barony of Talbotstown Lower, which derived its name from the Talbot family of Kilranaleagh in south Wicklow. (Map Terry Myler; origination by Nicholas Trant)

35 The Dublin Linen Hall opened in 1728 and was administered by the Linen Board, which promoted the Irish linen industry by guaranteeing the quality of the linen sold. Linen halls in Belfast and Newry were established in 1782 following a dispute between the northern suppliers and the Linen Board. By the beginning of the nineteenth century the industry was increasingly concentrated in the northeast of the country. (Engraving by W Hincks from JR Green *A Short History of the English People*, vol I)

37 This etching was titled 'Jemmy O'Brien with his working tools' – a dagger for stabbing friends in the back and a Bible on which to swear their lives away. The gallows is a grim reminder of the results of his efforts. (Irish school, circa 1800, photograph courtesy of the National Gallery of Ireland)

38 Both before and after the Rebellion of 1798, anyone suspected of being a member of the United Irishmen was subjected to summary treatment. Floggings, half-hangings and pitch-capping were the favourite punishments. (*The Irish Magazine*)

39 James Gillray's colour aquatint of United Irishmen in training was published in June 1798. The rebels are depicted as sub-human peasants and their military dress and methods of training are intended to provoke a reaction of derision and fear. This was one of the first illustrations to set guidelines for the portrayal of the Irish – 'large grizzled jaws, bulging eyes, and wide margin between snub nose and thick upper lip'. (National Army Museum, London)

40-41 George Cruikshank (1792-1879) was a well-known English caricaturist and book illustrator. William Hamilton Maxwell's *History of the Irish Rebellion in 1798* (published in 1845) contains twenty-one etchings by Cruikshank, mainly of the conflict in Leinster. They follow the Gillray prototype – the rebels and supporters are ape-like louts, intent on looting, burning and killing; the soldiers and loyalist civilians are trim and deciplined.

42 Extract from John Finnemore's letter of claim: 'He had 900 guineas in Cash he got some of it back – A Man of the name of Lawlor came and told him Genl Reynolds a Rebel General wanted him, he refused to go – and a party came soon after and forced him away to Black-moorhill – he got away from them on the Thursday – he made enquiry immediately for his Servant Maid who had left his House, and found she was gone that Morning and that she had 2 Silver Ladles of his property, and that she had been heard in the night counting Money – that he had ordered 4 Men to follow her, and they overtook her on the road to Dublin, & they brought her back – That he asked her what she had got with her, she say'd she had some things for him, and she gave him two Purses containing 603 Guineas – denied having any thing more, but having charged her with the Ladles she took him to a Quarry where the Ladles were with some other articles of Plate and a Trunk full of clothes.' (NAI M.5513/4)

44 Originally owned by the Talbot family, supporters of King James 11, and forfeited after the Battle of the Boyle, Carton was bought in 1739 by the nineteenth Earl of Kildare for £8,000. He employed the German architect, Richard Castle, to build the present house. His son James, who became the first Duke of Leinster, married Emily, a

daughter of the second Duke of Richmond, and one of their sons was Lord Edward Fitzgerald of the United Irishmen. (From an engraving of a painting by George Petrie)

45 One of a pair of engravings, depicting College Green, Dublin, before and after the Act of Union. In 'After the Union', the bustle has been replaced by empty spaces, the fashionably dressed groups by beggars and squatters, the private carriages by hackney cabs. (From *History of Dublin,* by Sir John T Gilbert, Dublin 1903)

47 Russborough was designed by Richard Castle. The interior has fine stucco ceilings, the work of the Francini brothers. Acquired in 1952 by Sir Alfred and Lady Beit, it is now open to the public. (From an engraving of a painting by JP Neale, *Views of the Seats of Noblemen and Gentlemen in the United Kingdom,* London 1826)

48-49 Hal Smith's portrait was taken in his youth while Elizabeth's dates from the latter part of her long life — and it is recorded that she didn't care much for it! (His portrait courtesy Patricia Pelly, hers courtesy Patricia Pelly and Dermot James)

50 Ballyward House shows the substantial style in which large tenant farmers lived. The Finnemores, who were associated with Blessington since the time of Morough Boyle, son of the archbishop, were the most important tenants on the estate. The house is now owned by the Macauley family. (Photograph courtesy Jim Corley))

51-52 Indentures (or leases) of the eighteenth and nineteenth century on well-run estates such as those of the Downshires were elaborate documents, often with ornate lettering and intricate decoration of the opening sentence. (52 – courtesy Jim Corley; 53 – PRONI)

54 One of a series of maps of the estate undertaken at the request of Baroness Sandys. Many landowners had their estates surveyed and the resultant maps, often executed in water-colour, were very attractive. Between 1770 and 1860, Charles Dunbar of the Boyle family and the first, second and fourth marquises of the Hill family all commissioned maps of the estate (the third marquis, ever careful of expense, was the exception). This of 1804, by John Longfield, of Blessington Demesne and Deerpart (when Blessington House was in ruins), shows that despite the landscaping undertaken by the Downshires in the 1780s, many of the original features of Boyle's demesne can still be identified. These include the ponds and the avenue linking the house to St Mary's Church. Various fields are named; those closest to the Deer Park were called the bastion fields, while Munfine (Munfine), which once designated the entire area of Blessington, was consigned to a piece of bogland close to Dillonsdown. The map also shows that some of the demesne lands were being tilled while the out-offices adjoining the ruined house

were still in use. Longfield was based in Dublin and from 1799-1805 worked with the Downshire surveyor, Thomas Murray, who had an office at 64 Grafton Street, Dublin. In 1807 Longfield was working at 67 Grafton Street and later moved to 19 Harcourt Street. (PRONI D.671/M2/27. Copy courtesy of Margaret Gowen & Co)

55 The opening paragraph reads: 'My Lord – With heartfelt Pleasure and the utmost Sincerity do I offer my Congratulations upon your Lordship's having arrived at that Period when you can exercise the high Prerogatives attach'd to your exalted Rank: not, my Lord, for having the Power to dispose of a great Property, but of using those splendid Talents God has blessed you with for the Good of Mankind in general, and of our Country in particular: and, believe me, my Lord, I am both sincere and full of Faith when I pray that you may live many years a Wise and Just Counsellor of your King and an Ornament and Benefactor to your Country. Your Lordship's Munificence to the Poor Cottagers has made the Blessing of him that was ready to perish to come upon you and caused the Widow's Heart to sing for Joy....' (PRONI D.671/C/211/4)

56 The third marquis's letter to Rev Hill Benson, five months later, is short and to the point. It reads: 'As the accts delivered to Mr Handley at Blesinton were only made up to November 1807, it is my earnest wish that you should without loss of time make these up to the 1st of last November & then send these to Mr Crozier who will forward them to me, in order that I may see the state of the property, & who is in arrears, & that I may prevent in future any person from literally cheating me, & alleging excuses for the non payment of my right. I shall of course hold you answerable for the execution of my wishes, which can easily be done.' Hill Benson soon fell from favour and retired to Inch House near Arklow in east Wicklow. (PRONI D.671/C/211/11 and 13)

57-58 When Henry Gore died, his widow and family had to vacate the agent's house at very short notice; there is no further mention of the family in the estate papers but one member – Honora Gore, who married James Moore of Burgage – remained and her descendants still live in Blessington. Two daughters of William Owen lived in Edmondstown, outside Blessington, until the 1940s. (Anvil Books)

59 The valuation map is based on Griffith's Valuation. Also known as the Primary Valuation, it was a countrywide survey undertaken between 1848 and 1860 by Naas-born engineer Sir Richard Griffith. It provided the basis for the calculation of rates to finance the Poor Law (which had been introduced in 1838) and took place in the Blessington area in 1853. The survey was produced in printed volumes and showed the occupants of land and houses, and the area

and value of the holdings. (Maps Terry Myler; origination by Nicholas Trant)

62-63 There was an enormous difference in the living standards of tenants in nineteenth-century Ireland. For some tenants in the upland areas of the Blessington estate, conditions might not have been dissimilar to those depicted in the sketch of a west of Ireland cabin during the Famine. For the more prosperous tenants in the lowlands, well-maintained houses with furniture, cooking utensils and even the luxury of pets would have been the norm. (62 – *The Illustrated London News;* 63 – John Mulvany *Well-off tenants – interior scene,* photograph courtesy of the National Gallery of Ireland)

64 The tender, which was not successful, reads:' I, Joseph Tallent (on second consideration) do propose to give for that farm of land in Hempstown (lately held by Mr Foley) the yearly rent of 42s 0d per Irish acre, also to pay in hand all arrear due on above farm or 50s 0d exclusive of all arrear. Dated this 8th day of April 1841.' The Tallons (or Tallents as the family was usually referred to in estate papers) were well-established tenants on the estate, holding over 60 acres in Threecastles at this time. Tallons first appeared on the rentals in 1817 but were probably there much longer as undertenants of George Ponsonby. In 1827, Michael Tallon was one of the few Catholic tenants on the estate who obtained a lease. Michael's sons, Garret and Joseph, farmed 59 and 90 acres respectively and their descendants lived there until the the early decades of the twentieth century. When Thomas, Garret's son, died, he left the land to his brother Patrick, a priest in America. In the latter's memoirs, he recalled that he had had 'a normal education' supplemented by a private tutor in the evenings. The family were bacon factors and in the 1850s and 1860s supplied 'Wicklow ham' to the Dublin and English markets until it was superseded by Limerick ham. They also exported cattle to Norwich where they were fattened for sale. (Information from Janet Halligan, Oldcourt, and PRONI D.671/C/230/52)

65 George Begley held a 50-acre farm in Threecastles throughout the nineteenth century. His neighbours were Tassie, Wilson and Cooke on the south side of the river Liffey and Patrickson on the north. The Tassie family held a farm of 200 acres in Threecastles and were involved in stone quarrying at Goldenhill; a lane known as Tassie's Lane once linked the Kilbride–Threecastles road with the Oldcourt road. (PRONI D.671/M2/31)

66 John Murray's letter to the third marquis in June 1837 emphasised the difficulty of collecting rents. Extract: 'The rents from the mountain part of the Lordship are coming in slowly. There is some

reason for it. The cattle are very poor in condition and the sheep as yet not shorn. I have put keepers on Brocky, Ballynatona, Blackrock and Bsmuttan, for if a tenant is unable to pay by any cause, the others hold back but that must not be allowed. I have rec(eived) lst, 2ⁿᵈ and 3ʳᵈ (rent day) £440. I expect good payment on Monday and the following days.' (PRONI D.671/C/214/342)

67 A lease of 180 acres in Crosscoolharbour, granted in 1772 to a William Fearis, was by the early decades of the nineteenth century divided among three members of the Fearis family. In 1837, Peter Fearis, who held 80 acres, was threatened with losing a large portion of his holding because of arrears, which, as on other holdings on the estate, had accumulated during an agricultural depression two decades earlier. Murray, under pressure from the Hillsborough administration, obviously felt he had to make an example of Fearis. The latter appealed, over his head, to the third marquis and this is one of four letters written by him. It starts: 'My Lord – 'With much pain I respectfully write to your Lordship. My little hereditary tenement under your Lordship is <u>so</u> dear to me – I pay full value for it full as Much as I can Make of it without even a Sufficiency of the essential comforts that hard work and human nature requires....' (PRONI D.671/C/218/1)

68 A contemporary sketch illustrates the congestion that came from subdividing small plots of land. (*The Illustrated London News*)

69 After the granting of Catholic Emancipation, O'Connell's next objective was Repeal of the Union. To enlist support he organised mass meetings all over the country. (*The Illustrated London News*)

70 This sketch of Blessington showing St Mary's Church and the agent's house (now the Downshire Hotel) was used as an embellishment to a map of the estate made in 1857 by Robert Manning at the request of the fourth marquis. (PRONI D.671/M2/32)

71 John Longfield's 1806 map of Blessington identifies the occupants of the houses and shows that the layout of the town was as we know it today. (Adapted by Nicholas Trant from the original. PRONI D.671/M2/27)

72 Patrick Kearney, who built the Market House, was under fire from the third marquis because of delays and faulty workmanship. Defending himself, he quotes Parry, the Downshire accountant, as saying the job was 'a real pattern of work and so well as you done it, so well in proportion you will merit by it'. He ended his letter with the softener, 'If I live to see you in ten years to come you will be a different man to what you now are, and you were well enough the first day I seen you.' The marquis scrawled across the bottom: 'Very handsome of him.' (PRONI D.671/C/227/6)

73 The Church of Our Lady of Mercy (1857) was built on the site of an older church dating from the 1770s. According to tradition, the original church was incorporated into the new building but there was no disruption of services while the work was in progress. (Kathy Trant)

74 Nimmo's bridge was a highly romantic concept, with parapets and turretted watch-towers. (Old engraving)

75 The mill at Blessington, an integral part of the lives of the tenants in the nineteenth century, was submerged when the reservoir was formed at the end of the 1930s. Kathleen Brophy, a teacher in Lacken in the 1920s, cycled past the mill daily on her way to work and did a painting of it in later life; it is now in the possession of Vincent Byrne, whose grandfather, Edward Moore, was one of the last occupants of the mill house. (Drawing Terry Myler, based on the Brophy painting)

79 The Society of Friends (Quakers) soup kitchen in Cork, set up to relieve distress during the Famine. (*The Illustrated London News*)

81 Tenants who got a rent reduction in the first winter of the Famine signed a receipt for the amount. If they could not write, their mark was accepted. (PRONI D.671/V/322)

82 Of the tenants listed, within two years all but two families had been evicted and by 1854 only one tenant was left in the townland. (PRONI D.671/R2/79)

83 When tenants left or were evicted, the roof of their cabin was invariably torn off to ensure that there would be no reoccupation. (*The Illustrated London News*)

84 and 86 Charles Lever's novel, *The Martins of Cro'Martin*, illustrated by "Phiz" was published in 1856, which places the sketches near enough to the Blessington scene of the 1840s and 1850s. (Chapman and Hall, London 1856)

89 From left to right: Patrick Egan, TD Sullivan, Charles Stewart Parnell, Thomas Sexton, the reporter, WH O'Sullivan, Thomas Brennan, Joseph Biggar, Tim Healy. (*(The Illustrated London News)*

93 The *Leinster Leader* had a readership in counties Kildare, Carlow and Wicklow. The report of 1 April 1882, covering an eviction and a sheriff's sale of cattle, is typical of the type of coverage given in the nationalist press to events during the Land War. (*Leinster Leader*)

95 The monument commemorating the coming of age in December 1865 of the Earl of Hillsborough was erected, according to the inscription, by the grateful tenantry. The Market House was built by the third marquis. (The National Library of Ireland)

98 Under the Encumbered Estates Act of 1849, creditors could force the sale of estates that were heavily in debt.

Sources for other illustrations

Archive prints: 36, 43, 88, 92
Green, John Richard, *A Short History of the English People*: 4, 5, 6, 9
Halls' *Ireland*: 61
Hillsborough Castle – Harrison Photography: 85
Hulton Picture Library, 18, 90,
The Illustrated London News: 53, 77, 78, 80, 87, 91, 94
Irish Compendium (Thomas Ransom, London 1753): 15, 16, 28, 29
Knight, Charles, *The Popular History of England:* 10, 11, 25, 26
Myler, Terry: 46, 96, 97
The National Portrait Gallery, London: 14 (Isaac Oliver, 1565-1617);
    32 (artist unknown);
    33 (miniature by Richard Cosway after a painting by Pierre Conde);
    60 (etching by Thomas McLean after a painting by Richard
    Dighton)
PRONI, 76

🕮 Bibliography

Primary Sources

Bodleian Library, Oxford
Rawlinson MS: Boyle to his son, Morough, Viscount Blessington, Dublin, 15 and 22 November 1690 (C. 984 folios 85-6).

British Museum, London
Ormond Papers: Boyle to Ormond, Dublin, 18 March 1678 (Additional MS 34,772); microfilm in NLI (positive 772).

Dublin Diocesan Archives
Troy Papers: Rev Roger Miley to Archbishop Troy, Blessington, 4 June 1798 (AB 2/116/7).

Irish Architectural Archives, Dublin
Blessington House building contracts and accounts: Archbishop Boyle's contracts and accounts with Lucas and Browne, 1671-5, copies of originals in private hands (89/18).

National Archives Ireland, Dublin
Finnemore, family: claim by John Finnemore for damages sustained in rebellion of 1798, 25 January 1799 (M 5513/4).

Miley, Rev Edward: sale of land at Tinode, county Wicklow, 10 March 1806 (M 5679).

Moore, George Ogle: abstract of title to an estate in Kilbride, county Wicklow, c.1830 (M 5690).

Official Papers: Commission for Enquiring into Losses Sustained by Loyalist in 1798 Rebellion, July 1799 –June 1803 (61/4 and 150/4).

Record Commission: Claims of Losses Sustained by Suffering Loyalist in 1798 Rebellion (RC 14/10).

Relief Commission: correspondence regarding Famine relief in Blessington, July 1846 – February 1847 (RLFC 3/1/3073 and 3/2/32/35 and 36).

State of the Country Papers: malicious damage to property belonging to Rev Michael Donnellan (SOC 2374/34).

National Library of Ireland, Dublin
Census of Ireland, 1841 and 1851.

Coolattin Emigration Books, 1847-1856 (MS 4974-5).

de Vesci MSS: rent roll of the estate of the Archbishop of Armagh (Michael Boyle), 1678, microfilm (positive 6797).

Genealogical Office, Boyle Pedigree, MS 161.

Griffith's Valuation: Primary Valuation of Tenements, Talbotstown Lower Barony, 1853.

Historical Manuscripts Commission: Boyle to Sir John Percivale, Cork, 29 May 1660, Egmont MSS (vol 1, 1905: 611); Boyle to Thomas Osborne, 1676, Leeds MSS (Rep 11, App 7, 1888:12); Boyle to Lady Ranelagh, Dublin, 14 April 1679 and Boyle to Ormond, the Lord Deputy, Blessington, 17 August 1678, Ormond MSS (Rep 6, App, 1877:735 and 743).

Journals of Elizabeth Smith, 1840-1885 (MS 36,220/1-20): *see also* Pelly and Tod (1991) and Thomson and McGusty (1980).

Ordnance Survey Names Book, Wicklow.

Papers in Private Hands

de Robeck Estate Papers: copies of some of the material on microfilm in NLI (positive 7143-4 and 7161).

Finnamore lease for Ballylow.

Public Record Office of Northern Ireland

Downshire Papers (Index available in NLI (special list 300-1):

– correspondence: (a) first and second marquis and Baroness Sandys, 1746-1809 (D.607); (b) third marquis and the Hillsborough officials, 1809-1845 (D.671/C/211-231).

– guardian, executors and trustees accounts: 1874-78 (D.671/A18).

– lease documents: individual leases from the seventeenth to end of nineteenth centuries (D.671/L2 and LE2), lease books compiled in 1794,1802 and 1876 summarising tenure (D.671/A4).

– maps and plans: includes estate maps drawn up at the request of Charles Dunbar, the first, second and fourth marquises and Baroness Sandys, 1770-1880 (D.671/M2 and P2).

– minute-books: summary of estate policy and practice, 1813-28 (D.671/A5).

– rentals: includes financial statements of monies paid from the rentals, such as, annuities, payment to employees, expenses incurred improving the estate, allowances to tenants and contributions to various charities, 1810-1908 (D.671/R2).

– rental arrears: list of tenants in arrears with observations, 1885 (D.671/A34/21).

– title-deeds to the estate and other legal papers: includes the granting of the land in Blessington to Michael Boyle, the town charter, and various legal documents such as wills, mortgages, legacies, covenants, maps, surveys and election writs, 1667-1778 (D.665 and D.671/D2).

– Valuation book: notes by Brassington and Gale and Robert Manning's report, 1861-1867 (D.671/A33/1).

– vouchers: includes signed receipts of individual tradesmen and labourers and Wynn's report of 1881, 1783-1891 (D.671/V).

Index available in NLI (special list 300-1):

Representative Church Body, Dublin
Combined Register of Baptisms, Marriages, Burials and Vestry Minutes of Blessington Parish, 1683-1879 (P.651/1/1).

Works of Reference
Brogan, E and A Kilfeather (1997) *Archaeological Inventory of County Wicklow,* Dublin: Government Publications.

Connolly, SJ (ed) (1999) *The Oxford Companion to Irish History,* Oxford: Oxford University Press.

Doubleday, HA and H de Walden (eds) (1936) *Complete Peerage,* vol IX, London: St Catherine's Press.

Gibbs, V (ed) (1912) *Complete Peerage,* vol II, London: St Catherine's Press.

Lewis, S (1837) *Topographical Dictionary of Ireland,* Dublin.

Stephen, L and S Lee (eds) (1917) *Dictionary of National Biography,* vols II, IX and XVI, Oxford: University Press.

White, G (ed) (1949) *Complete Peerage,* vol XI, London: St Catherine's Press.

Secondary Sources

Bardon, J (1992) *A History of Ulster,* Belfast: Blackstaff Press.

Barry, J (1982) *Hillsborough, a Parish in the Ulster Plantation,* Belfast: Mullan and Son Ltd.

Bartlett, T (1994) 'Masters of the Mountains: the Insurgent Careers of Joseph Holt and Michael Dwyer, County Wicklow, 1798-1803' in K Hannigan and W Nolan (eds) *Wicklow, History and Society,* Dublin: Geography Publications.

Belfast Protestant Journal, 19 April 1845.

Belfast Newsletter, 25 April 1845.

Boyce, DG (ed) (1988) *The Revolution in Ireland 1879-1923,* Dublin: Gill and Macmillan.

Brady, J (1963) *In Monavalla,* Dublin: Gill and Son.

Brady, J and A Simms (eds) (2001) *Dublin Through Space and Time,* Dublin: Four Courts Press.

Bull, P (1996) *Land, Politics and Nationalism,* Dublin: Gill and Macmillan.

Butler, P and P Kelly (2000) *The National Concert Hall,* Dublin: Wolfhound.

Campbell, SJ (1994) *The Great Irish Famine,* Strokestown: Famine Museum.

Canny, N (1982) *The Upstart Earl,* Dublin: Cambridge University Press.

Christian Brothers, Monkstown (2000) 'Brief History of Monkstown Park', www.iol.ie/cbcmonks/history.

Comerford, RV (c.1995) 'Co Kildare and the Famine' in *Lest We Forget: Kildare and the Great Famine,* Kildare County Council.

Connell, KH (1950) *The Population of Ireland 1750-1845,* Oxford: Clarendon Press.

Corlett, C and J Medlycott (eds) (2000) *The Ordnance Survey Letters, Wicklow,* Wicklow: Roundwood & District Historical & Folklore Society, Wicklow Archaeological Society and Kestrel Books.

Craig, M (1980) *Dublin 1660-1860,* Dublin: Figgis.

Craig, M (1989) *The Architecture of Ireland from the Earliest Times to 1880,* London/Dublin: Batsford/Eason.

de Paor, L (1986) *The People of Ireland,* London: Hutchinson.

de Breffny, B (1989), 'The Building of the Mansion at Blessington', *IAR:* 73-7.

Donnelly, B (1994) 'From Grand Jury to County Council: an Overview of Local Administration in Wicklow 1605-1898' in *Wicklow History and Society,* Dublin: Geography Publications.

Donnelly, JS (1975) *The Land and the People of Nineteenth-Century Cork,* London: Routledge and Kegan Paul.

Dooley, T (2000) 'Landlords and the Land Question, 1879-1909' in C King (ed) *Famine, Land and Culture in Ireland,* Dublin: University College Dublin Press.

Dooley, T (2001) *The Decline of the Big House in Ireland,* Dublin: Wolfhound Press.

Freeman's Journal, 14, 19 and 24 April 1845.

Fleming, WEC (2001) *Armagh Clergy 1800-2000,* published by author in conjunction with Dundalgan Press.

Flower, R (1978) *The Western Island,* Oxford: Oxford University Press.

Foster, RF (1988) *Modern Ireland 1600-1972,* London: Allen Lane.

Green, ERR (1949) 'A Catalogue of the Estate Maps in the Downshire Office', *UJA,* vol 12: 1-25.

Green, ERR (2001) 'The Great Famine 1845-50' in TW Moody and FX Martin *The Course of Irish History,* Cork: Mercier Press.

Guinness, D and W Ryan (1971) *Irish Houses and Castles,* London: Thames & Hudson.

Handcock, WD (1991) *The History and Antiquities of Tallaght,* Dublin: Anna Livia Press.

Hall, SC and AM (c.1840) *Ireland, Its Scenery & Character etc,* London.

Hannigan, K (1994) 'Wicklow Before and After the Famine' in *Wicklow History and Society,* Dublin: Geography Publications.

Hill, Lord George (1846) *Facts from Gweedore,* Dublin; republished by Institute of Irish Studies, Queen's University Belfast, 1971.

James, D and S Ó'Maitiú (1996) *The Wicklow World of Elizabeth Smith, 1840-1850,* Dublin: Woodfield Press.

Johnson-Liik, EM (2002) *History of the Irish Parliament, 1692-1800,* Belfast: UHF.

Kildare Observer, 17 January, 26 and 28 February and 27 March 1880, 27 August 1881.

Leinster Leader, 18 and 21 January, 11 February, 11 March, 1 and 8 April 1882; 8 October 1998.

Longfield, AK (1945) 'Linen and Cotton Printing at Stratford-on-Slaney, Co Wicklow' in *RSAIJ,* vol LXXV: 24-31.

Longworth Dames, RS (1893) 'Miscellanea', *RSAIJ,* vol III: 430-1.

Lyons, FSL (1973) *Ireland Since the Famine,* Glasgow: Collins/Fontana.

Lyons, FSL (1968) *John Dillon,* London: Routledge and Kegan Paul.

Lyons, FSL (1982) *Culture and Anarchy in Ireland 1890-1939,* London: Oxford University Press paperback.

McCall, H (1881) *The House of Downshire,* Lisburn and Belfast.

McCartney, D (2000) 'Parnell, Davitt and the Land Question' in C King (ed) *Famine, Land and Culture in Ireland,* Dublin: University College Press.

Maguire, WA (1972) *The Downshire Estates in Ireland 1801-1845,* Oxford: Clarendon Press.

Maguire, WA (1993) 'Owners and Occupants' in *Hillsborough Castle,* UAHS.

Maguire, WA (ed) (1998) *The 1798 Rebellion in Ireland,* Belfast: UM.

Maguire, WA (ed) (1998) *Up in Arms,* Belfast: UM.

Malcomson, APW (1978) *John Foster: the politics of the Anglo-Irish Ascendancy,* Oxford: University Press.

Malcomson, APW (1981) 'The Gentle Leviathan: Arthur Hill, 2nd Marquis of Downshire, 1753-1801' in P Roebuck (ed) *Plantation to Partition,* Belfast: Blackstaff Press.

Martin, FX *The Course of Irish History,* Cork: Mercier Press.

Mitchell, F (1986) *The Shell Guide to Reading the Irish Landscape,* Dublin: Country House.

Moody, TW (2001) 'Fenianism, Home Rule and the Land War: 1850-91' in TW Moody and FX Martin *The Course of Irish History,* Cork: Mercier Press.

Mooney, P (1989) *Tallaght: History and Legend,* private publication.

Myers, S and D McKnight (eds) (1995) *Sir Richard Musgrave's Memoirs of the Irish Rebellion of 1798,* Indiana: Round Towers Books.

Nichols, F (1745) *Irish Compendium: or Rudiments of Honour,* London: J & P Knapton.

Nolan, W (1994) 'Land and Landscape in County Wicklow' in *Wicklow History and Society,* Dublin: Geography Publications.

O'Brien, M and C (1985) *A Concise History of Ireland,* London: Thames & Hudson.

O'Connor, J (1995) *The Workhouses of Ireland,* Dublin: Anvil Books.

O'Donnell, R (1994) 'The Rebellion of 1798 in County Wicklow' in *Wicklow History and Society*, Dublin: Geography Publications.

O'Donnell, R (1998) *The Rebellion in Wicklow 1798*, Dublin: Irish Academic Press.

Ó Gráda, C (1989) *The Great Irish Famine*, Dublin: Gill and Macmillan.

Ó Gráda, C (1995) *Ireland, A New Economic History 1780-1939*, Oxford: Clarendon Press.

Ó Maitiú, S and B O'Reilly (1997) *Ballyknockan: A Wicklow Stonecutters' Village*, Dublin: Woodfield Press.

O'Neill, TP (1973) 'Fever and Public Health in Pre-Famine Ireland', *RSAIJ*, vol 103: 1-34.

O'Neill, TP (2000) 'Famine Evictions' in C King (ed) *Famine, Land and Culture in Ireland*, Dublin: University College Dublin Press.

Ó Tuathaigh, G (1984) *Ireland Before the Famine 1798-1848*, Dublin: Gill and Macmillan.

Pakenham, T (1972) *The Year of Liberty*, London: Panther.

Pelly P and A Tod, (1991) *The Highland Lady in Ireland*, Edinburgh: Canongate Classic.

Póirtéir, C (ed) (1995) *The Great Irish Famine*, Cork: Mercier.

Price, L (1953) *The Placenames of Wicklow*, Dublin: Institute of Advanced Studies.

Reilly, E (2000) 'Brief History of Blessington Demesne', www.mglarc.com/projects/ blessington.

Roche, R (1995) *The Norman Invasion of Ireland*, Dublin: Anvil Books.

Sadlier, T (1928) 'The Manor of Blessington', *RSAIJ*, vol XVIII: 128-31.

Smith, WJ (1985) 'Explorations of Place' in J Lee (ed) *Ireland Towards a Sense of Place*, Cork: University Press.

Stewart, ATQ (2001) *The Shape of Irish History*, Belfast: Blackstaff Press.

Stokes, G T (1893) 'The Antiquities from Kingstown to Dublin', *RSAIJ*, vol III: 343-56.

Taylor, R (undated) *History of St Mary's Church*, Blessington: St Mary's Parish.

Thomson, D and M McGusty (eds) (1980) *The Irish Journals of Elizabeth Smith 1840-1850*, Oxford: Clarendon Press.

Tillyard, S (1995) *Aristocrats*, London: Vintage.

Trant, K (1997) 'The Landed Estate System in the Barony of Talbotstown Lower in the Nineteenth Century', unpublished MA thesis, NUI, Maynooth.

Vaughan, WE (1994) *Landlords and Tenants in Mid-Victorian Ireland*, Oxford: Clarendon Press.

Wakefield, E (1812) *An Account of Ireland, Statistical and Political*, London.

ℒ Index

(Numbers in italics refer to illustrations. Names on the 1850 List of Tenants in the Appendix are only indexed if a connection can be made with the text).

Kathy Trant, born in Tullow, county Carlow, has strong family ties with Wicklow and has lived in the Blessington area for the past three decades. She became aware of the richness of the archival sources on the Blessington area some years ago while undertaking post-graduate research. The book results from her desire to make this material available to a wider audience. Kathy is married and has four children and two grandchildren.